FIFTY YEARS
HONOURING CANADIANS

BY THE SAME AUTHOR

On Her Majesty's Service: Royal Honours and Recognition in Canada

The Maple Leaf and the White Cross: A History of St. John Ambulance and the Most Venerable Order of the Hospital of St. John of Jerusalem in Canada

The Beginners Guide to Canadian Honours

Canadian Symbols of Authority: Maces, Chains, and Rods of Office

Commemorative Medals of The Queen's Reign in Canada, 1952–2012

Savoir Faire, Savoir Vivre: Rideau Club, 1865–2015

The Canadian Honours System, 2nd Edition

FIFTY YEARS
HONOURING CANADIANS

The Order of Canada, 1967–2017

CHRISTOPHER McCREERY

Foreword by Jean Vanier, CC, GOQ

DUNDURN
TORONTO

Printer: Friesens

Library and Archives Canada Cataloguing in Publication

McCreery, Christopher, author
        Fifty years honouring Canadians : the Order of Canada, 1967-2017
/ Christopher McCreery ; foreword by Jean Vanier, CC, GOQ.

Includes bibliographical references and index.
Issued in print and electronic formats.
ISBN 978-1-4597-3657-3 (hardback).--ISBN 978-1-4597-3658-0 (pdf).--
ISBN 978-1-4597-3659-7 (epub)

1. Order of Canada--History. 2. Decorations of honor--Canada--History. I. Vanier, Jean, 1928-, writer of foreword II. Title.

CR6257.M321 2017   929.8'171   C2016-905937-5
                                                     C2016-905938-3

1 2   3   4   5   21 20   19   18   17

We acknowledge the support of the **Canada Council for the Arts** and the **Ontario Arts Council** for our publishing program. We also acknowledge the financial support of the **Government of Ontario**, through the **Ontario Book Publishing Tax Credit** and the **Ontario Media Development Corporation**, and the **Government of Canada**.

Care has been taken to trace the ownership of copyright material used in this book. The author and the publisher welcome any information enabling them to rectify any references or credits in subsequent editions.
                                                     — *J. Kirk Howard, President*

The publisher is not responsible for websites or their content unless they are owned by the publisher.

Printed and bound in Canada.

VISIT US AT

 dundurn.com | @dundurnpress | dundurnpress |  dundurnpress

Dundurn
3 Church Street, Suite 500
Toronto, Ontario, Canada
M5E 1M2

To the more than six thousand members of the Order of Canada who have worked so diligently to "desire a better country," thereby enhancing the lives of countless millions.

Her Majesty Queen Elizabeth II,
Sovereign of the Order of Canada.

It seems to me that the Order of Canada, which honours distinguished service by Canadians from every region and walk of life, should add to our sense of togetherness by giving recognition and honour to those who have served the whole realm.

— The Rt. Hon. Roland Michener, Governor General
and first Chancellor of the Order of Canada, November 7, 1967

The Rt. Hon. Roland Michener,
PC, CC, CMM, OOnt, CD, QC.

CONTENTS

FOREWORD	By Jean Vanier, CC, GOQ	11
INTRODUCTION		13
ONE	Debate and Discord: Honours in Canada	15
TWO	A Nascent Idea	29
THREE	Out of the Optimism of the 1960s	37
FOUR	Establishing a National Institution	45
FIVE	The Path to Appointment	63
SIX	The First Investiture and Dinner	71
SEVEN	Expansion and Evolution: Reform and the Birth of the Chancellery	77
EIGHT	Special Events, Investitures, and Anniversaries	93
NINE	The July 1922 Crew: Butler, Beatty, and Bryant	107
TEN	Insignia and Symbols of the Order	119
ELEVEN	Crafting a Token of Recognition: Manufacturing the Insignia	137
TWELVE	Centrepiece of an Honours System	145
ACKNOWLEDGEMENTS		151
NOTES		152
BIBLIOGRAPHY		159
IMAGE CREDITS		161
INDEX		163

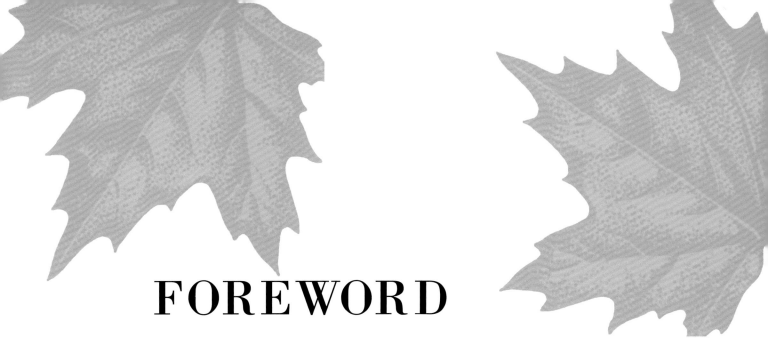

FOREWORD

As we approach the 150th anniversary of Canadian Confederation, those of us who are old enough recall the many celebrations of the Centennial year that were held across the country, including the extraordinary Expo 67 in Montreal. One of the great legacies of that year was the establishment of the Order of Canada. Little did we know then that this Canadian honour would become one of our country's most cherished institutions. For fifty years, Canadians who have "desired a better country" have been recognized for their achievements in many fields as well as for service to their communities, the nation, and the world.

For my family, 2017 is also the fiftieth anniversary of the death of my father, Georges Vanier, who was then the governor general of Canada. While he did not live long enough to be invested into the Order that he helped establish, my mother, Pauline, was among the inaugural Companions of the Order of Canada in recognition of her humanitarian works. My parents committed their lives and abilities to the service of others at home and abroad. When they were recognized for their service, they were conscious of the many people with whom they served who shared in the honours they received.

To my surprise, I was appointed an Officer of the Order of Canada (then called the Medal of Service) in 1971 for my work founding the community of L'Arche in Trosly-Breuil, France. I accepted this recognition on behalf of L'Arche and of the men and women who had helped me to create this small community, where people with and without intellectual disabilities could share life together and grow in friendship and freedom. For me this recognition was not the end of the road, but an encouragement to go further. In the coming years, L'Arche would expand to Canada, India, and a further thirty-five countries around the world. In 1971, the organization Faith and Light was formed, and has since brought their vision of belonging for persons with disabilities and their families to over eighty countries. In 1986, I was promoted to Companion of the Order of Canada in recognition of the growth of L'Arche and Faith and Light.

The thousands of people who have been recognized by the Order of Canada, some of whom I count among my friends, are an amazing group of people — talented, generous, and committed. Some of these men and women have brought their gifts to their local communities, while others have been of service to the country or to the world. In each case, the honour they have received is shared by the many thousands of men, women, and children who have worked with them, both in their particular endeavours and in the effort of building a better world. It is no wonder that Canadians have embraced the Order of Canada.

I salute my fellow members of the Order, and enjoin them to continue their good works and service. Membership in the Order of Canada is a tremendous honour, but it is also a responsibility to represent what it means to be a Canadian and to inspire others to join in building a better future for all people.

Jean Vanier, CC, GOQ

INTRODUCTION

The fiftieth anniversary of the establishment of the Order of Canada is an opportune moment to reflect upon the excellence and scope of achievement that our national fellowship of honour has sought to recognize. More than six thousand Canadians have been recognized with the distinctive snowflake insignia. Their story is the story of Canada's progress and development in modern times.

Weaving together the story of the Order of Canada along with images associated with the history of the Order, this scrapbook of the Order's history provides a pictorial journey through the signal moments in the Order's life and evolution. Rich with artifacts from the history of the Order, this work provides the most comprehensive pictorial history of the Order yet assembled. Containing everything from images of the Order's first insignia and ribbon, to programs from the inaugural investiture, and photos of those who played a central part in establishing the Canadian honours system, this work brings together the foundational elements that have been key to the Order's establishment and evolution.

The history of honours in Canada is by no means one driven by the state; rather it is the product of various people and their personalities, desires, vanities, and, in a few cases, vision. Canada's relationship with honours from the end of the First World War through to the creation of the Order of Canada in 1967 is a story of controversy, discontent, and obfuscation that was ultimately overcome by a small group of people who possessed a vision for a Canadian honours system. This system was created as a mechanism through which the Crown could recognize outstanding citizens for their contributions in the local, national, and international spheres. Key amongst these people was Vincent Massey, the first Canadian-born governor general since the French regime. Massey spent much of his adult life promoting the concept of a uniquely Canadian honour. Certainly part of this quest for a Canadian order was driven by his own desire to be recognized — but much more profound was his sense that the country as a whole would benefit greatly from an institution that recognizes the great and the good of the land — through a non-partisan and equitable system of honours. Massey, along with Lester Pearson, Gordon Robertson, Michael Pitfield, Esmond Butler, and John Matheson, and others who played subtler roles, including Bruce Beatty, Joyce Bryant, and John Halstead, all contributed to the establishment of the Order of Canada and, by extension, the broader Canadian honours system. These were the lead players in a larger cast of actors in the drama that unfolded as Canada struggled to deal with the question of honours and recognition. A chapter has been devoted to the builders who had the longest association with the Order. Also included are sixteen vignettes of those who played a role in the Order's establishment: small windows into their lives and the specific role that they played in the establishment of our national Order.

The overall structure of the book is based on a 2013 exhibition catalogue published by the Musée de la Légion d'honneur et des ordres de chevalerie, *De Gaulle et le Mérite: Création d'un ordre républicain*, on the occasion of France's Ordre national du Mérite's golden anniversary. The first eight chapters trace the Order of Canada's history chronologically, while the last four deal with matters related to some of the key contributors to the Order's development, and such symbolic issues as the insignia and physical representations of the Order.

This work is not intended to provide an exhaustive history of the Order of Canada or the Canadian honours system — rather its purpose is to offer an overview of how the Order of Canada came to be established, touching upon the rancorous debates that surrounded honours in Canada for half a century before 1967. Those seeking an in-depth study of honours should consult the second editions of *The Canadian Honours System* and *The Order of Canada: Genesis of an Honours System*, the two most detailed histories of honours in Canada.

ONE

DEBATE AND DISCORD:
HONOURS IN CANADA

Almost every sovereign nation around the globe has an honours system, which is quite simply an official way for the state, on behalf of the people, to recognize outstanding contributions, meritorious service, bravery, military service, and long service. Despite the ubiquity of honours systems, Canada went nearly fifty years without civil honours to recognize the sort of contributions that are today acknowledged through the Order of Canada. The story of how Canada abandoned civil honours is one that plays a significant role in the development of the grassroots-nominated, non-partisan model of honours pioneered with the establishment of the Order of Canada in 1967.

The Order of Canada and broader Canadian honours system finds some of its origins in the honours systems of two of Canada's founding peoples: the French and the British. Canada's indigenous peoples did not have a formal honours system; however, they did have a well-defined concept of honour. Service to a community and bravery were recognized in indigenous communities not with gold or silver medals but through respect accorded to individuals, often through the adoption of chieftainship. Amongst the Inuit, a different system existed through a system of rewards, akin to honours. Military achievement was occasionally rewarded by "distinctive facial tattoos."[1] With the arrival of Europeans, this system was augmented through the awarding of Chief's Medals, which French and British officials used to recognize the loyalty of a particular indigenous group or the achievement of a treaty. These medals continue to be presented to this day on special occasions.

Indian Chief Medal.

Charles Le Moyne, Seigneur de Longueuil, Baron de Longueuil.

Pierre de Rigaud.

Honours were seldom conferred in New France, despite the fact that prior to the French Revolution France had an extensive honours system. It was a system graded by the hierarchy of French society. The sovereign would elevate French subjects to the nobility as dukes, marquises, counts, viscounts, and barons. One Canadian, Charles Le Moyne, Seigneur de Longueuil, was made Baron de Longueuil in recognition of his peace negotiations with the Iroquois on behalf of the French Crown. In New France, honours were awarded by the governor on behalf of the King — however honours could not be conferred without the approval of the King. The principal honour bestowed upon those living in New France was the Ordre royal et militaire de Saint-Louis, which was established by Louis XIV in 1693. The Order consisted of three grades: Grand Cross (limited to eight members), Commander (with a limit of twenty-four members), and Knight (with no limit on the overall membership). It was an honour conferred for distinguished military service, and one limited to Roman Catholic men alone. Notable French governors such as Louis-Hector de Callière; Louis de Buade, Comte de Frontenac; and Pierre de Rigaud, Marquis de Vaudreuil-Cavagnal, were amongst the Order's Canadian members.

Perhaps the most well-known subject in New France to receive the Order of St. Louis was François Coulon de Villiers. Coulon de Villiers went on to serve in the French

Commander of the Order of St. Louis.

King Louis XIV of France.

colonial army with great distinction. In the battle for Fort Necessity, on July 4, 1757, Coulon de Villiers became the only man to ever defeat George Washington in battle. Following the fall of New France in 1759, the British honours system supplanted its French predecessor as the principal means by which Canadian residents were recognized for distinguished military and, later, public service.

Until 1967, Canada used the British honours system, what are more accurately referred to as "imperial honours," for all military and civil honours. As in Royal France, these honours included being made a duke, marquess, earl, viscount, or baron. These are the various degrees of the peerage — hereditary titles which entitle the holder to sit in the British House of Lords. The hereditable quality of these titles would later cause problems in Canada. Baronetcies are not part of the peerage but are hereditary titles, the holders of which do not sit in the House of Lords but use the title "Sir." Then there were the orders of chivalry, such as the Order of the Bath (Knight Grand Cross, Knight Commander, and Companion), the Order of St. Michael and St. George (Knight/Dame Grand Cross, Knight/Dame Commander, and Companion), and eventually the most accessible honour, the Order of the British Empire (OBE), which had five levels (Knight/Dame/ Grand Cross, Knight/Dame Commander, Commander, Officer, and Member). The higher

Knight Commander of the Order of St. Michael and St. George.

The Military Cross, a senior gallantry decoration for the army.

The Distinguished Flying Cross, a senior gallantry for members of the RCAF.

Commander of the Order of the British Empire.

King George V, the sovereign who created Canada's first honour, the RCMP Long Service Medal.

levels of those orders (Knight/Dame Grand Cross and Knight/Dame Commander) carry knighthood, which means the person is dubbed a knight and assumes the non-hereditary title of "Sir" or "Dame." In addition to these honours for meritorious military and civil contributions, there was a host of gallantry awards and bravery decorations, such as the Victoria Cross, Distinguished Conduct Medal, Military Cross, Distinguished Flying Cross, Military Medal, and George Medal to name a few. There were also a variety of medals for war service were awarded to Canadians for service in the South African War, 1899–1902, First World War, and Second World War.

Canadians came to administer these honours and the Canadian government had control over who received them, although most of the same orders, decorations, and medals were used throughout the British Empire/Commonwealth. Given the large number of Canadians who received imperial honours during the last century — well over two million when one considers the various service medals awarded for the First and Second World Wars alone — it would be revisionist to pretend that these honours were "foreign." In Canada, honours administration was left to the prime minister, who was allotted a certain number of knighthoods for which he could recommend Canadians to be appointed to. While the sovereign was — and remains — the fount of all honours, the prime minister once had an immense degree of personal control over who received honours, whereas today he or she has no formal influence over who is recognized with Canadian honours. Aside from a few very high-profile cases, the Canadian government once had a great degree of control over the flow of British honours. Nevertheless, the perception remained that imperial honours were tightly controlled by the British government.

The Crown has always been the "font of all honours" in Canada, and this requires that all officially recognized honours be created by the sovereign and either awarded in the name of the Queen or sanctioned by the Crown. Following Confederation, a convention emerged whereby the prime minister of Canada submitted his honours lists to the governor general, who vetted them and submitted them to the colonial secretary and then on to the sovereign. The governor general, who was at that time a British official, also nominated Canadians for honours, usually without the knowledge of the Canadian prime minister. Awards for members of the military were submitted by the Department of Militia and Defence to the governor general for transmission to London.

From the turn of the century through to the end of the First World War, a series of public scandals related to honours brought the topic to national prominence and resulted in much debate in the press and Parliament. The first of these controversies arose over the knighting of Thomas Shaughnessy, president of the Canadian Pacific Railway. The governor general, Lord Minto, suggested to the prime minister, Sir Wilfrid Laurier, that Shaughnessy be knighted in view of his services during the 1901 Royal Tour of the Duke and Duchess of Cornwall and York (the future King George V and Queen Mary). Laurier opposed the idea on the grounds that Shaughnessy was unpopular with Canadians and certainly no friend of the prime minister or the Liberal Party. The governor general, however, disregarded Laurier's advice and advanced the nominations to the King.

The Duke and Duchess of Cornwall and York departing Parliament, 1901.

Sir Wilfrid Laurier addressing members of the Royal Tour Party in front of the Parliament Buildings, 1901.

Laurier was furious when Shaughnessy was knighted, and it did not help that he learned of the appointment from a newspaper and not his governor general. In response to this incident, Laurier drafted an official policy on honours in Canada. It set out that all honours, except the Royal Victorian Order, had to be approved by the prime minister of Canada before any list could be sent from the governor general to the King. While this proposal was coldly received by the governor general and British officials, they did eventually agree that the prime minister of Canada should be involved in reviewing the honours lists and submitting names, emulating the practice in the United Kingdom. Nevertheless, the imperial authorities maintained that the governor general would retain the right to nominate Canadians for honours.

It was the First World War that brought the issue of honours to a head. The war brought much social and constitutional change to Canada and this included the nation's policy toward honours. Prior to the war, there had been only muted opposition to titular honours such as peerages and knighthoods. Honours were viewed as necessary, even if they were used as tools of partisan patronage from time to time. This prevailing attitude changed during the war as a result of several high-profile controversies. In particular, two very public scandals over honours induced Parliament to examine the issue.

Sir Wilfrid Laurier.

Lord Minto, a keen supporter of imperial honours in Canada.

Cartoon of Sir Wilfrid Laurier after he accepted his knighthood in 1897.

The first involved the 1915 appointment of the inept Canadian minister of militia and defence, Sam Hughes, as a Knight Commander of the Order of the Bath. Hughes had been pilloried in the press over his overall administration of the department of militia and defence and the Canadian Expeditionary Force. Sir Sam's bombastic approach, cronyism, and problematic procurement of the Ross Rifle were widely reported.

The more serious outrage occurred in 1917 when Sir Hugh Graham, owner of the *Montreal Star* and a staunch imperialist, was made a member of Britain's House of Lords, taking the title Lord Atholstan. This appointment was made against the advice of the Canadian prime minister and governor general. Graham's peerage was controversial in part because of his highly controversial right-wing views. Although an unpopular figure, Graham had built up a major newspaper and founded a number of other publications.

This was the only time in Canadian history that the British government simultaneously ignored formal advice from both a governor general and the Canadian prime minister. The disregard of the Government of Canada's wishes was related to the fact that the British prime minister, David Lloyd George, was selling peerages and knighthoods to raise funds for his political party. While the use of honours to reward political contributions was hardly new, under Lloyd George such transactions had become particularly blatant and highly developed with an actual schedule of fees linked to specific peerages and honours.

In addition to the Hughes and Graham controversies, there was an underlying naïveté about honours in Canada. Peerages and knighthoods were thought to be the same thing — both hereditary — and there was similar confusion about other honours. For instance, when the establishment of the Order of the British Empire was announced in 1917, Canadian newspapers pronounced that three hundred Canadians were going to be knighted with the new Order. This was certainly not the case.

As a result of Graham's peerage, Sir Robert Borden drafted a new government policy, through Order-in-Council 1918-668, setting out that all honours must be approved by the Canadian prime minister and that no further hereditary honours (peerages or baronetcies) were to be conferred on Canadians.

Ye Arms of Ye Honorable Sam.

DUM · SPIRO · BLATERO

IT has long been the editorial conviction of this publication that so doughty a champion as Major-General (antedated two years) the Honorable Sam Hughes should have a coat-of-arms befitting his martial prowess. SATURDAY NIGHT, therefore, set the Toronto Branch — or Lodge or Local, or whatever they call it — of the Royal College of Heralds at work. The picture which accompanies this notice is the result of their labors. And here is the description in proper heraldic language of the various quarters of the suggested escutcheon:

"ARMS, quarterly—1st. Gules, between two Chevrons, or, an Ass proper, rampant, armed argent; 2nd, Azure, on a bend, or, three Megaphones sable; 3rd, Azure, a Laurel Wreath, or, bound by a scroll bearing the motto, 'Mine by Mine Own Hand'; 4th, Argent, between two Harpoons, palewise, proper, a Whale blowing, sable.

"Crest—On a Mushroom, argent, a Cap and Bells, proper."

For the benefit of the uninitiated—after all, Heraldry is a rather unfamiliar art—it may be explained that "an Ass proper, rampant," is very much the same thing as "a proper Ass on the rampage." The Heralds suggested that for this figure there might be substituted "an Ass's Head erased," if the course of political history in this country should call for such a change. In this connection it may be pointed out that on the Hughes escutcheon—"an Ass's Head erased"—would be good heraldry and good common-sense.

The meaning of the motto, "Dum Spiro Blatero," must be fairly obvious, even to such readers of SATURDAY NIGHT as may have forgotten the Latin they learned at school. It means, "While I breathe I blather." The appropriateness of the line must be at once evident.

Only a week after this policy was drafted, William Folger Nickle, the Conservative-Unionist MP for Kingston, introduced a resolution in the House of Commons requesting that the King cease awarding peerages to Canadians. Nickle had no trouble with knighthoods or other honours, only those that had a hereditary quality. Nickle's resolution was, in fact, very similar to Borden's new policy. After lengthy debate, the House of Commons adopted a resolution placing power over recommendation for all honours in the hands of the Canadian prime minister, while at the same time asking the King to cease conferring hereditary titles to Canadians.

This is what came to be known as the Nickle Resolution, even though Nickle himself voted against the version eventually adopted by the House.

Sir Robert Borden.

Above: A copy of Borden's Order-in-Council, which attempted to place control over honours in the hands of Canadian authorities.

Right: Image of the temporary House of Commons Chamber where the Nickle Debates transpired.

Although the Nickle Resolution was adopted, the debate was far from over. While military honours continued to be awarded, Borden did not send forward any further recommendations for civilian honours. Throughout late 1918 and most of 1919, the British press was filled with reports about people purchasing peerages and knighthoods. Although this was a problem confined to Britain, many people in Canada assumed that the same practice was followed on this side of the Atlantic as well. Fearing that an avalanche of knighthoods was to accompany the newly created Order of the British Empire, Nickle introduced another motion in April 1919. This one called for the King to "…hereafter be graciously pleased to refrain from conferring any titles upon your subjects domiciled or living in Canada." Nickle was now pursuing a prohibition on all titular honours, a departure from his original opposition to only hereditary honours. Following another lengthy debate that in many ways mirrored the one in 1918, the House of Commons voted to create a Special Committee on Honours and Titles. The committee held several meetings and eventually submitted a report to Parliament that called for the King to cease conferring all honours on residents of Canada, except military ranks and vocational and professional titles. The committee approved of the continuance of naval and military decorations for valour and gallantry. The final part of the report affirmed the committee's desire to see that no resident of Canada be permitted to accept a title of honour or titular distinction from a foreign (non-British) government. The Commons passed a motion of concurrence with the report and it was adopted.

There has, invariably, been confusion about the Nickle Resolution and the Report of the Special Committee on Honours and Titles. Neither was a statute, and neither had any standing as anything more than a recommendation or guideline, as Prime Minister R.B. Bennett would demonstrate in 1933. The Nickle Resolution served as a policy document on how a prime minister could submit honours lists, and while it requested that no further hereditary honours be bestowed, it did not prevent Canadians from accepting other honours, whether a knighthood or appointment to the Order of the British Empire.

William Folger Nickle, father of the Nickle Resolution.

William Lyon Mackenzie King shortly after his investiture as a Companion of the Order of St. Michael and St. George.

Neither Prime Minister Arthur Meighen nor his successor William Lyon Mackenzie King submitted honours lists, and there were no honours conferred between 1918 and 1933. It would be Canada's Depression-era prime minister, R.B. Bennett, who would revive imperial honours in Canada, albeit with some significant modifications.

It is worth noting that the prohibition on Canadians accepting honours was not universal. Canadians living in other parts of the Empire were still eligible to be awarded honours. In 1925 Canadian-born Emma Albani, the world-renowned soprano and the first Canadian to attain international stardom as a result of artistic abilities, was honoured with a damehood. Albani was made a Dame Commander of the Order of the British Empire in 1925, the first Canadian woman to be so honoured, but as she resided in the United Kingdom, the Canadian government did not become involved in her appointment. Another prominent example was that of Dr. George Washington Badgerow, a distinguished ear, nose, and throat doctor. Badgerow was born and trained in Canada, although he made his home in Britain and went on to be knighted in 1926, without any protest from the Government of Canada.

Prime Minister R.B. Bennett broke the moratorium on honours that had existed in Canada between 1919 and 1933. In fact, Bennett adhered perfectly to the Nickle Resolution and had eighteen Canadians knighted and 189 appointed to the various non-titular levels of the imperial orders of chivalry. Bennett solicited nominations from the various lieutenant governors and other officials and then personally selected each candidate. Unlike previous lists, Bennett's were non-partisan and well distributed amongst the provinces and between both sexes — quite a novelty for the period. At 48 percent proportionally, more women were recognized with honours in Bennett's lists than have yet been recognized in the modern Canadian honours system. Among the most notable people honoured in Bennett's lists were Sir Frederick Banting, the co-discoverer of insulin;

Sir Ernest MacMillan, the noted composer and conductor; Sir Thomas Chapais, the esteemed historian; Sir Edmund Wyly Grier, the portrait artist; and Sir Arthur Doughty, the Dominion archivist. At the non-titular level, Lucy Maud Montgomery was made a Commander of the Order of the British Empire and Lester Pearson was made an Officer of the Order of the British Empire. For the first time, women represented nearly half of those being recognized with honours. Public reaction to these awards was muted.

Richard Bedford Bennett, the prime minister who pioneered the concept of honours to recognize exemplary citizenship and non-partisan contributions at all levels of Canadian society.

Further comment on the return of titles after 15 years of absence. (March 16, 1934.)

A political cartoon deriding Bennett's reintroduction of honours, c. 1934.

Sir Frederick Banting, KBE, MC, perhaps the most famous Canadian knighted as part of R.B. Bennett's revival of civil honours in Canada.

It was also during this period that the first honour created by the King as sovereign of Canada, was established on the advice of his Canadian government.

In March 1934 George V created the Royal Canadian Mounted Police Long Service Medal, which was awarded to members of the RCMP who had served twenty years of long service with good conduct. This first Canadian honour continues to be part of our modern honours system. Bennett was the last Canadian prime minister to make use of all aspects of the imperial honours system. Following his departure from public office, Bennett moved to Britain and achieved his childhood dream of sitting in the House of Lords when he was made Viscount Bennett in 1941.

When William Lyon Mackenzie King was returned to office as prime minister in 1935, the brief revival of imperial honours came to an end. Thus, Canada entered the Second World War with no honours system at all, and no policy on honours, other than that there were to be none, aside from those conferred for long service in the RCMP and Canadian military. Following the outbreak of the Second World War, it was none

The RCMP Long Service Medal, obverse and reverse, c. 1937.

other than George VI who raised concerns about the inability of his Canadian sailors, soldiers, and air personnel to receive honours for their gallantry and meritorious service in defence of freedom. The special Awards Coordination Committee (ACC) was struck in Ottawa. This committee drafted formal honours policies to allow for Canadians to receive gallantry decorations, and later also permission to be recognized for meritorious service in aid of the war effort at home and overseas.

As will be discussed in the following chapter, throughout the Second World War numerous proposals were devised to create a Canadian order, but none came to fruition. Thus Canada continued to work within the broader imperial honours system. In 1942 Parliament again tackled the issue of honours and awards. The committee proposed that the Canadian government should establish a Canadian order of merit. From 1942 through to 1948, numerous proposals were advanced for the creation of a Canadian order of merit. These carried such names as the Royal Order of Canada, the Royal Elizabethan Order, the Order of the Beaver, the Canadian Decoration of Honour, the

George R.I.

George the Fifth, by the Grace of God, of Great Britain, Ireland and the British Dominions beyond the Seas King, Defender of the Faith, Emperor of India, to all to whom these Presents shall come, Greeting:

WHEREAS it is Our desire to reward the long and meritorious service of members of Our Royal Canadian Mounted Police:

We do by these Presents for Us, Our Heirs and Successors, institute and create a new Medal to be awarded to any duly qualified Officer, Non-Commissioned Officer or Constable of Our Royal Canadian Mounted Police in accordance with the following rules and ordinances:

Firstly, - It is ordained that the Medal shall be designated and styled "The Royal Canadian Mounted Police Long Service Medal".

Secondly, - It is ordained that the Royal Canadian Mounted Police Long Service Medal shall consist of a circular Medal of Silver, one and a half inches in diameter, with Our Effigy on the obverse, and on the reverse, the Crest and Motto of Our Royal Canadian Mounted Police, surrounded by the legend "For Long Service and Good Conduct",

Thirdly, - It is ordained that the riband of the Medal shall be of Royal Blue with two yellow stripes

The Royal Warrant establishing the RCMP Long Service Medal.

Canadian Award of Honour, the Order of Canada, the Order of St. Lawrence, and the Canada Medal. This latter award, the Canada Medal, was established in 1943; however, at the insistence of Prime Minister William Lyon Mackenzie King, the medal was never awarded. In the absence of an order of Canada, Canadian service personnel and civilians were made eligible for the non-titular levels of the Order of the Bath, the Order of St. Michael and St. George, the Order of the British Empire, and the Imperial Service Order. This, too, came to an end with the conclusion of the war, and Dominion Day 1946 saw the last civil honours list until the establishment of the Order of Canada.

With the outbreak of the Korean War, the government was once again faced with making decisions about honours in Canada. It decided to institute a policy similar to that used during the Second World War, which allowed for members of the Royal Canadian Navy, Canadian Army, and Royal Canadian Air Force to accept imperial gallantry decorations and the non-titular levels of the imperial orders of chivalry. No provision was made to allow for Canadian civilians working in aid of the war effort to be recognized with honours, and thus the drought of honours for Canadian civilians continued. In 1956 a new policy was adopted, which allowed both Canadian civilians and military personnel to be recognized with imperial gallantry awards, but no provision was made for any honours to be conferred in recognition of meritorious service of any type.

TWO

A NASCENT IDEA

The idea behind creating the Order of Canada was not new, nor did it simply spring out of the enthusiasm and energy of Canada in the 1960s. It was Lord Bathurst, Britain's colonial secretary, who first proposed the establishment of a Canadian order in 1823. This was likely inspired by the 1818 creation of the Order of St. Michael and St. George specifically for Malta and the Ionian Islands. His proposal did not progress past the stage of a rough concept, however, as George IV disliked the idea of creating separate orders for each of his overseas colonies. This attempt was followed nearly fifty years later when Lord Monck, Canada's first governor general, made a similar suggestion, again inspired by the 1861 creation of the three-levelled Order of the Star of India. Monck's proposal also called for three levels: Knight Grand Cross of the Order of St. Lawrence (GCSL), Knight Commander of the Order of St. Lawrence (KCSL), and Companion of the Order of St. Lawrence (CSL). As with other imperial orders of chivalry, the top two levels would have conferred knighthood, and thus the recipient would have become "Sir Jonathan Shanks, KCSL."

One cannot help but speculate whether Canada would have discarded titular honours had a Canadian order of chivalry been created at that time. The Colonial Office was not willing to allow the new Dominion to create such a potent symbol of national autonomy, and thus Canada continued to work within the existing imperial honours system.

Viscount Monck, Canada's governor general, 1867–68. Monck attempted to create a Canadian knighthood, the Order of St. Lawrence.

LEFT: Vincent Massey, as a young diplomat in Washington, D.C. Throughout his life, Massey lobbied for the creation of a Canadian honour.

RIGHT: William Lyon Mackenzie King, the killjoy of Canadian honours.

The Royal Order of Canada design proposed by Charles Comfort.

The origins of the Order of Canada as we know it today can clearly be traced back to Vincent Massey. His persistence and ideas played a central role in the creation of a uniquely Canadian honour, which he initially styled the Order of St. Lawrence, based on Monck's old idea. Massey, in many ways the first Canadian diplomat, would go on to be a long serving Canadian High Commissioner to London and then be appointed the first Canadian-born governor general since the French regime. He was keenly interested in the development of Canadian culture, symbols, and the Canadian nation in the widest sense.

Massey first broached the subject in 1935 with the newly installed governor general, Lord Tweedsmuir, who was very keen on encouraging the creation of Canadian institutions and subsequently brought the subject up with his prime minister William Lyon Mackenzie King. Mackenzie King was annoyed with the proposal and Massey dropped the issue for a period of time. Canada's longest-serving prime minister had a phobia when it came to honours, going as far as to ask the British government to cancel his appointment as a Companion of the Order of St. Michael and St. George more than thirty years after he received it. This did not prevent him in later life from accepting the Commonwealth's premier non-titular award, when he was appointed to the Order of Merit in 1947, and a number of foreign awards, making him the most highly decorated Canadian prime minister to date. Mackenzie King was the proverbial killjoy when it came to honours in Canada.

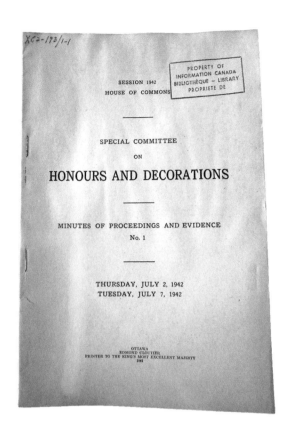

Cover of the 1942 Parliamentary
Report that called for the establishment
of a Canadian honour.

Throughout the war, the Awards Coordination Committee met regularly to discuss the
issue of honours in Canada. While the committee's task was primarily to develop policy in
relation to imperial honours being bestowed upon Canadians, it would often delve into the
subject of creating a Canadian order. To this end, between 1941 and 1946 it submitted no
fewer than five different proposals to the prime minister. Each was in turn rejected. In 1942
a special parliamentary committee, the Special Committee on Honours and Awards, called
for the creation of a Canadian order, a recommendation that was also ignored. It was at this
time that the actual name "Order of Canada" originated, as part of Massey's proposal for a
Royal Order of Canada — although it was the under-secretary of state, Ephriam Coleman,
and the secretary to the governor general, Major-General H.F.G. Letson, who simplified
the name to the Order of Canada. This name persisted in proposals until the creation of
the Order of Canada in 1967, although other designations, ranging from the Order of the
Beaver and the Order of St. Lawrence to the Royal Elizabethan Order, were also suggested.

Despite the failure of its various proposals, the ACC did manage to have the Canada
Medal established in 1943. It was a curious award, to say the least, as it was to be awarded
to everyone from army privates to heads of state. While extensive lists of recipients were
composed, the medal was never awarded. Mackenzie King wanted nothing to do with
honours, especially the Canada Medal; in his mind, the existing imperial honours system,
though flawed, worked well in Canada, and he had no desire to make forays into the
honours debate by creating a Canadian system.

The Canada Medal, obverse and reverse.

In 1948 the governor general, Lord Alexander of Tunis, proposed to the prime minister that, at long last, an order of Canada be established — conveniently, he borrowed much of the proposal from one initially made in 1945. In a letter to his prime minister, Lord Alexander wrote: "Personally I am very much in favour of the institution of an order of Canada, in possibly five degrees this order could be along the lines of the U.S. Legion of Merit."[2] Lord Alexander suggested that the Order of Canada consist of five levels:

- Grand Commander of the Order of Canada GCOC
- Grand Officer of the Order of Canada GOOC
- Commander of the Order of Canada COC
- Officer of the Order of Canada OOC
- Member of the Order of Canada MOC[3]

Alexander went further, noting that "it would seem to me that Canada, as a sovereign nation, should have its own order, and that this development would now follow logically the recent official recognition of a distinctive Canadian citizenship."[4] A most perceptive analysis of the situation, but Mackenzie King had no interest in pursuing the matter and politely turned it aside. The country would have to wait nearly two more decades before an order of Canada would be established — but that did not stop various people from continuing the quest to establish a national order.

As part of the seminal report of the Royal Commission on the National Development of the Arts, Letters and Sciences (what became known as the "Massey Commission"), a detailed proposal for the establishment of a Canadian order was included. Harkening back to Lord Monck's proposal, Massey again proposed an Order of St. Lawrence, this time with five levels:

- Grand Commander of the Order of St. Lawrence (GCSL)
- Grand Officer of the Order of St. Lawrence (GOSL)
- Companion of the Order of St. Lawrence (CSL)
- Officer of the Order of St. Lawrence (OSL)
- Member of the Order of St. Lawrence (MSL)

Field Marshal Viscount Alexander of Tunis. Alexander was anxious to see Canada adopt the symbols of full nationhood.

Most significantly, Massey proposed that the honours list for this new order be composed by a non-partisan committee, quite unlike the practice that had previously been followed in Canada and Britain, where the prime minister had a direct influence over the flow of honours. Although the proposal was given to the leaders of the opposition parties, it failed to gain the approval of then–prime minister Louis St. Laurent, who was in part concerned about sanctioning the creation of an order that bore a name so similar to his own. One can only imagine the reaction of St. Laurent's political adversaries to the establishment of an order serendipitously bearing the prime minister's name.

Members of the Massey Commission: Arthur Surveyor, Vincent Massey, Norman Mackenzie, Father Georges-Henri Lévesque, and Hilda Neatby.

RIGHT: The Massey Commission Report.

BELOW: The Canadian Forces' Decoration, established by King George VI in 1949 to recognize long service in the Canadian Armed Forces.

ROYAL COMMISSION ON NATIONAL DEVELOPMENT IN THE

arts, letters & sciences

PRICE $3.50

Following the failure of the Massey Commission's proposal for an Order of St. Lawrence in 1951 and into the 1960s, it was the Department of National Defence (DND) and a few senior Ottawa bureaucrats that maintained the pressure for an order of Canada to be established. For members of the Canadian military, there had been few new ribbons to decorate their chests following the Korean War. Members serving twelve years received the Canadian Forces' Decoration.

There were a number of UN medals for service in Egypt, Yemen, and the Congo, and an international medal for work in Vietnam, but that was the extent of the honours available. Unlike all of Canada's NATO allies, Canada had no general medals for service in specific areas and there were no awards for meritorious service. At the 1959 and 1960 annual meetings of the Conference of Defence Associations (CDA), resolutions were put forward calling for the establishment of a system of honours.[5] In October 1959 the Department of National Defence began to review the 1948 Lord Alexander proposal for an order of Canada. Officials in the department noted, "From time to time, citizens of Canada, whether as civilians or as members of the Navy, Military and Air Forces, render valuable and meritorious service above and beyond their normal duties, which service is worthy of special recognition."[6] The associate minister of national defence, Pierre Sévigny, was supportive and a meeting of the Government Decorations Committee was called to consider the proposal.

On March 11, 1960, the West Block of Parliament was the site of the meeting of the Decorations Committee, the successor body to the Awards Coordination Committee. The committee came to some pretty profound conclusions at their meeting and recommended that the existing government policy toward honours be changed "so as to permit the awarding of decorations or honours for other than war service and gallantry (war and non-war)."[7] It went on to propose the creation of a Canadian order of chivalry to recognize the aforementioned service. "The new order should be awarded only in recognition of exceptionally valuable and meritorious service to Canada above and beyond the normal duties which service is worthy of special recognition."[8] It seemed that the country was finally going to establish a national honour; the Order of Canada was on the cusp of being created.

Ten days after this very productive meeting, a letter classified as SECRET was sent to all members of the committee, "The Chairman of the Decorations Committee desires me to inform you that he has been asked by the Associate Minister of National Defence to ensure that the subject of the meeting of the committee held on Friday, March 11, 1960, will continue to be regarded as secret and confidential. The Chairman … has asked me to remind you of the importance of continuing to observe careful precautions of secrecy in the matter referred to."[9] This directive was sent out to all members of the committee after Prime Minister Diefenbaker learned of the plans and ensured the entire project was quickly shelved.[10] The "Chief" was as phobic about honours as was Mackenzie King. Diefenbaker's consent to delve into the subject of honours had not been sought. During the governor general's monthly meetings with the prime minister, Georges Vanier, well aware of the proposal for an order of Canada, enthusiastically raised the topic of honours in a supportive manner. Esmond Butler, secretary to the governor general, who dealt with the aftermath of the meeting, would later recount "when the Governor General mentioned this idea to Mr. Diefenbaker at a meeting, there was an explosion and the whole thing collapsed."[11]

There would be no more movement on honours until Diefenbaker was voted from office and replaced by Lester B. Pearson. While he was initially focused on replacing the Canadian Red Ensign with a new flag, he would eventually turn his energies to creating a national honours system, with the Order of Canada as its centrepiece.

John G. Diefenbaker, who quashed an attempt in 1960 to establish an Order of Canada.

VINCENT MASSEY, PC, CH, CC, CD (1887–1967)

There has perhaps never been a person in Canadian public life who so persistently sought to encourage the creation of a national honour as did Vincent Massey. Well beyond being covetous of such recognition, Massey was anxious to see that his fellow citizens were recognized for their good works. An ardent Canadian nationalist who used his position and personal wealth to encourage the development of the arts and educational institutions, following his service as Canada's first minister to Washington, D.C., and then as Canada's High Commissioner to the United Kingdom (1935–46), Massey went on to chair the Royal Commission on the National Development of the Arts, Letters and Sciences, better known as the Massey Commission. This report not only made proposals related to higher education and the development of the Canadian arts community, but also proposed the establishment of a Canadian order to be known as the Order of St. Lawrence. While this proposal was suppressed by the government, Massey would continue to encourage successive prime ministers to take action and establish a national order that would include a non-partisan based model of selecting members. As the first Canadian-born governor general, Massey undertook a robust program of outreach and involvement in all regions of the country. It was Massey's persistence and vision that brought about the Order of Canada that we know today, most notably the concept that the distribution of honours — "who gets what and why" — should not be controlled by politicians. He would be one of the first Companions of the Order of Canada, appointed in 1967. He died a little more than a month after his investiture.

THREE

OUT OF THE OPTIMISM
OF THE 1960s

Undaunted by Diefenbaker's grandiloquent reaction to the attempt to create an order of Canada, the under-secretary of state Jean Miquelon advanced a proposal for a commemorative medal to mark the centennial of Confederation, which would take place in 1967.[12] In 1959 the Centennial Commission was established by the federal government and extensive plans were already underway to mark the nation's hundredth birthday.

Canada had long followed a tradition of awarding medals at the time of the coronation of a new sovereign and also when the King or Queen marked an important jubilee. This had previously occurred during the reigns of Victoria, Edward VII, George V, George VI, and Elizabeth II, so the tradition was well established. While Canada had never before issued a commemorative medal for its birthday, the idea most likely came from India and Pakistan. When these two countries attained their independence, the British government arranged for special commemorative medals to be struck. Similarly, other countries in the Commonwealth had issued independence medals, so there was a well-established precedent.

Through 1963 and 1964, the idea of establishing a centennial medal continued to be discussed. In the intervening period, the government had changed and the Liberal Party had come to power under the leadership of Lester B. Pearson. The new government was anxious to adopt new symbols and, on January 22, 1964, Paul Hellyer, the recently appointed minister of national defence, approved the creation of the Centennial Medal. The only problem was he lacked the authority to direct the establishment of an official honour of the Crown!

The King George V Silver Jubilee Medal, the first widely distributed civil honour to be conferred on Canadians. More than 7,500 would receive it in 1935.

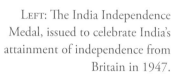

Left: The India Independence Medal, issued to celebrate India's attainment of independence from Britain in 1947.

Right: The Queen Elizabeth II Coronation Medal, 1953. This medal would be awarded to 19,000 Canadians during the coronation year.

Below: Paul Hellyer, who championed the creation of a military honour and the Canadian Centennial Medal, 1967.

Hellyer was desperate to find something to give members of the armed forces. In December 1963 he had begun developing a proposal to reorganize the Royal Canadian Navy, Canadian Army, and Royal Canadian Air Force. By early 1964 his plans to unify the three services into a single force were more fully developed — with significant opposition coming from senior members of the military.

Honours were once again being discussed, mainly because of the Centennial Medal. Hellyer and Secretary of State Gilles Lamontagne presented a joint memorandum to Cabinet on May 11, 1965. This memorandum outlined the insufficiency of the existing honours policy and concluded that the Centennial Medal would appropriately recognize "the specially valuable service of many Canadian citizens."[13] The submission was discussed at the Cabinet meeting on May 20, 1965, although the prime minister sidelined the proposal. "Mr. Pearson was inclined to the view that the institution of the Centennial Medal should be linked to the establishment of the Canada Medal."[14]

PRIME MINISTER · PREMIER MINISTRE

The Prime Minister of Canada presents his humble duty to Her Majesty The Queen.

It is desirable to provide for the establishment of a Canadian medal, as described in the accompanying memorandum, commemorative of the 100th anniversary of the Confederation of Canada, which may be conferred on Canadian citizens in recognition of their valuable services to Canada.

The Prime Minister, accordingly, humbly petitions Her Majesty graciously to approve the making of an Order by the Queen's Privy Council for Canada to make provision for the establishment of "The Canadian Centennial Medal, 1967".

The Prime Minister remains Her Majesty's most faithful and obedient servant.

Prime Minister of Canada.

Ottawa, May 30th, 1966.

ABOVE LEFT: The Queen's approval for the creation of the Canadian Centennial Medal, 1967.

ABOVE RIGHT: The Canadian Centennial Medal, 1967. Discussion surrounding this medal helped to spur Cabinet interest in honours. A total of 29,500 Canadians received this medal in 1967 for a diverse array of contributions and service.

The Centennial Medal was temporarily shelved, although it had the immediate impact of turning Pearson's mind to the idea of creating a Canadian honours system. This momentous project had been on Pearson's mind for some time — it was first introduced to him by Massey and was later pressed by fellow MP John Matheson prior to Pearson's election as prime minister.

In 1962 Matheson had encouraged Pearson to consider creating a Canadian honour.[15] After being elected in a May 1961 by-election, Matheson quickly became a friend and adviser to Pearson, eventually serving as his parliamentary assistant. While in New York visiting the United Nations with other parliamentarians, he found himself in the library of the UN headquarters. There, he began skimming through a variety of books about flags and honours. It was there that two ideas began to percolate. Having served as a captain in the Royal Canadian Horse Artillery during the Second World War, he was well acquainted with imperial honours and realized that Canada lacked a homegrown system. In the late 1940s, as a novice lawyer, he worked with W.F. Nickle in Kingston, Ontario. This was the same Nickle of Nickle Resolution fame who had brought the issue of titular honours to the floor of the House of Commons at the end of the First World War. He discussed honours with Nickle on a number of occasions, and he was influenced by his legal mentor's views on the topic. Nickle had never wanted to abolish all honours — only

John R. Matheson and George Stanley. Matheson served as Pearson's Parliamentary Secretary and, along with Vincent Massey, encouraged him to establish the Order of Canada. Matheson had previously been instrumental in the adoption of the national flag of Canada in 1965.

those which were hereditary or conferred a title. Nickle's egalitarian views on the subject would echo through the Order of Canada as it was finally created in 1967, especially with regard to the non-partisan nature of the order.

Pearson's interest in creating a national honour had almost certainly been sparked by Matheson in early 1962; however, he had another reason for wanting Canada to have its own honours system. Pearson had been made an Officer of the Order of the British Empire in 1934, and the story goes that his OBE was delivered to him over a fence while he was playing tennis![16] In a letter to then–Prime Minister R.B. Bennett, he expressed thanks for the honour, but asked for a raise in pay: "I cannot feed my family on an OBE alone."[17] Pearson stayed on at Canada House, home of the Canadian High Commission in London, for the early part of the Second World War; while there, he dealt with many questions about honours. This must have been among his most frustrating tasks. On the one hand, he was working for Vincent Massey, then High Commissioner, who was constantly promoting a Canadian order and the use of pre-existing imperial honours; the other side of the equation was Mackenzie King, who strenuously opposed all honours. Pearson was truly walking a tightrope — his career in the balance to some degree. While posted to the Canadian embassy in Washington, a deserving friend was overlooked in the 1943 honours list. Pearson recalled: "This is the sort of thing that makes a joke of Honours Lists. There is another defect in the list. Owing to the decision, a right one, not to permit titles, only junior decorations are available to Canadians on the list who, if they were in England, would probably receive the most senior ones…. The only way to avoid this is to establish our own Canadian Order."[18] An idea he first recorded in 1943 would eventually come to fruition, but not until Canada received a new symbol of nationhood — a new national flag.

Pearson had a long-standing interest in Canada adopting a new national flag. During the Suez Crisis, when the Canadian government announced its intention to contribute soldiers, the Egyptian government did not respond with enthusiasm. The Canadian flag was too similar to the British one. All of this had made President Nasser of Egypt suspicious.[19] As under-secretary of state for external affairs, and the lead architect of Canada's and the UN's contribution to calming the Suez Crisis, Pearson was deeply aware of the difficulties caused by the lack of a distinctive Canadian flag. This situation seems to have convinced Pearson that a new flag was necessary. His parliamentary secretary, Matheson, agreed with him.

LESTER B. PEARSON, PC, OM, CC, OBE (1897–1972)

The prime minister who put his political career on the line to see Canada adopt a new flag, Lester Pearson served from 1963–68 as Canada's leader, having previously served as secretary of state for external affairs and leader of Her Majesty's Loyal Opposition (1958–1963). It was in his role at external affairs where he was awarded the Nobel Peace Prize for his work on quelling the Suez Crisis. Pearson's own experience with honours as a soldier in the First World War, diplomat in the Second World War, and having himself been made an Officer of the Order of the British Empire in 1934, greatly coloured his views on the need for Canada to have its own system to recognize great citizens at the local, national, and international levels. Encouraged by his old friend Vincent Massey and a young MP, John Matheson, Pearson pressed forward with plans to establish an order of Canada. Although his initial desire for a three-level order was thwarted by Cabinet colleagues, within five years of its establishment, the Order of Canada that he envisioned came to take its modern form.

Matheson's visit to the UN library spurred him on with two projects. The first of these was not the creation of a Canadian order, but rather the creation of a new Canadian flag. The two projects were of monumental significance. Furthermore, they were intertwined: the adoption of a new Canadian flag on February 15, 1965, would greatly influence not only the desire to create a Canadian order, but also the very design of the insignia for that honour.

Without question, the flag debate was one of the most acrimonious the country had experienced since the Conscription Crisis of 1942. Successive prime ministers had attempted to deal with the question of creating a new Canadian flag. Mackenzie King had proposed a flag similar to the Red Ensign with a green maple leaf in the field; Bennett had proposed a Red Ensign with the word CANADA in the lower fly.[20] Neither prime minister was willing to press his proposal. St. Laurent, too, felt that Canada needed a distinctive flag, but he was more concerned with legislative changes to the country than with symbolic ones. Diefenbaker had no intention of adopting a new Canadian flag.

Pearson's Liberals came to power in 1963 having made the campaign promise of adopting a new Canadian flag within two years. Thousands of designs poured in to Parliament. A parliamentary committee was established and set about choosing a design, remaining mindful of the complex rules of heraldry. The design that was ultimately chosen remained true to Canada's heraldic traditions: it incorporated the national colours, red and white, as well as a stylized maple leaf. The maple leaf was a familiar symbol to Canadians, having been used during the First World War on the cap badges of the Canadian Expeditionary Force and on the first coins struck by the Dominion in 1871.[21]

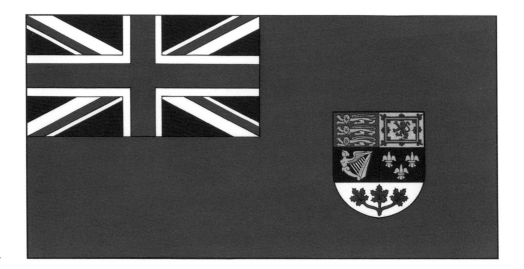

The Canadian Red Ensign, c. 1957.

The red-white-red pattern was taken from the flag of the Royal Military College (RMC),[22] which is said to have been based on the ribbon of the 1866–70 Canada General Service Medal. Matheson would recall that while visiting RMC, he had discussed the flag issue with George Stanley, RMC's dean of arts: "We had just emerged from the college mess and Dr. Stanley remarked, 'There, John, is your flag' … pointing to the Royal Military College flag flapping furiously [in the wind]."[23]

JOHN R. MATHESON, OC, CD, QC (1917–2013)

The man who would article with William Folger Nickle of Nickle Resolution fame, John Matheson served with distinction in the Royal Canadian Horse Artillery during the Second World War. A lawyer by training, Matheson would be elected as Liberal MP for Leeds, Ontario, from 1961 to 1968, later being appointed to the Ontario Court of Justice. Matheson was keenly interested in flags and honours and did much to focus Prime Minister Pearson's plan to replace the Canadian Red Ensign with a new flag. As Pearson's parliamentary secretary, following the successful conclusion of the flag debate, Matheson encouraged Pearson to press forward with establishing the Order of Canada. Along with Vincent Massey, Esmond Butler, and Michael Pitfield, Matheson would help lay the groundwork for the Order throughout 1966–67. He would be appointed an Officer of the Order of Canada in 1993.

The rest of the story is well known. After an exhaustive public and parliamentary debate,[24] the Maple Leaf flag, technically known as the national flag of Canada, was formally adopted on February 15, 1965. At last Canada had a distinctive flag, just in time for the Centennial in 1967. Pearson had other projects on his mind. He suggested that "O Canada" should be adopted as the national anthem and that Canada should establish a national honour. To these musings, one of his parliamentary colleagues responded: "Oh, my God, please don't. Haven't we had enough trouble about emblems? Please don't submit us to this."[25]

Temporarily, at least, Pearson was willing to set aside questions about anthems and honours. Nevertheless, Pearson did not completely lose interest in the honours question, and Matheson continued to encourage him, as

The Royal Proclamation of the National Flag of Canada, 1965.

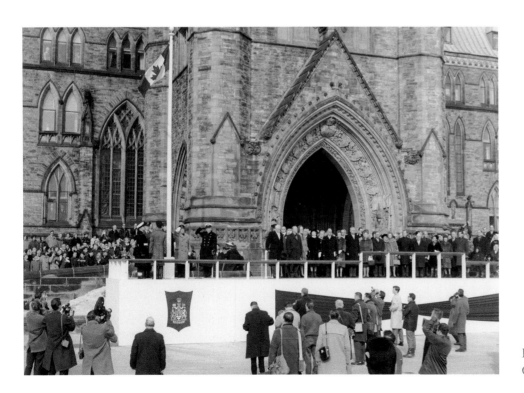

Raising of the new national flag of Canada, February 15, 1965.

Canada's new flag being raised in Halifax, Nova Scotia, 1965.

did his old boss from London, former governor general Vincent Massey. Pearson's initial plan was to use the order-in-council that had established the Canada Medal to create a new Canadian honour, but this was soon found to be an insufficient solution.

The much-maligned and ill-fated Canada Medal returned briefly to parliamentary debate on November 6, 1963, when Progressive Conservative member Marcel Joseph Aimé Lambert asked the government: "Have any awards of the Canada Medal been made since its institution in 1943?"[26] To this, Jack Pickersgill, the secretary of state, replied "no." It was curious that the recently dethroned Progressive Conservatives had suddenly gained an interest in honours, after nearly six years in power during which they could have arranged for its award.

The Canada Medal was examined one last time in Parliament on April 8, 1965, when Bill C-92 was introduced by Guy Leblanc, MP for Rimouski, Quebec. Leblanc noted that his bill was "to establish a distinctive Canadian decoration for the recognition of meritorious service by citizens of Canada or of other countries."[27] This bill received first reading but died on the order paper when Parliament was dissolved in advance of the 1965 general election. That election returned Pearson's Liberals to power, and the prime minister's mind turned to a new legislative program. The election had not delivered a majority, but it had reinvigorated him, and he set about planning for the upcoming parliamentary session.[28]

FOUR

ESTABLISHING A NATIONAL INSTITUTION

Having survived the political scandals and difficulties of 1965, Prime Minister Pearson began to make discrete enquiries about the possible structure of a Canadian order. During the Christmas break, he withdrew a number of books on the subject from the parliamentary library. By the end of January 1966, he contacted Vincent Massey, and the two had a detailed conversation about honours and the need for a system in Canada. Pearson asked Massey to re-examine the *Confidential Report on Honours and Awards* submitted by the Royal Commission in 1951.[29] After reviewing his old report, Massey suggested a few minor changes.

CLOCKWISE, FROM THE BOTTOM RIGHT: Massey, Vanier, Pearson, and John Ross McLean from the Canadian High Commission in London. Massey, Pearson, and Vanier would play an instrumental role in establishing the Order of Canada.

With more than thirty years' experience lobbying for the establishment of a Canadian honour, Massey cautioned the prime minister that many would criticize any attempt to create a Canadian order. He also foresaw that such an institution could be undemocratic if it was not carefully developed. He reminded Pearson that most of the people receiving awards in France and Britain were from "very modest walks of life … and in most countries are 'little people.'" Massey postulated that beyond the local level, "such a system in Canada would make, I think, a definite contribution to Canadian unity." Notwithstanding the possible roadblocks, Massey's enthusiasm was obvious: "I shall be glad at any time to talk about this problem with you. For years I have felt that we should do something towards the establishment of an honours system in Canada. I think the matter has very great importance. Please call on me if I can be of any help."[30]

Realizing the complexity of the project and the time it would require, Pearson asked his parliamentary secretary John Matheson "to look into this important matter."[31] Matheson commenced detailed research at the Library of Parliament and began dissecting Massey's 1951 proposal.

On March 8, Massey received a call from Matheson. Impressed, Massey cabled the prime minister suggesting that Matheson visit him at Batterwood — Massey's country home near Port Hope, Ontario — "quite soon."[32] Pearson dispatched Matheson to Batterwood[33] to meet with the one true expert on the subject. On March 16, Matheson arrived at Batterwood and stayed for just over a day. Massey remained excited — for the first time, a prime minister was taking an active interest in what he considered "his" subject — and he wrote to the governor general's secretary, Esmond Butler, that "we are making progress!"[34]

Lester B. Pearson (left) and Georges Vanier (right), friends from their days at the Canadian High Commission in London. One of Vanier's last official acts was to sign the Order-in-Council, authorizing the establishment of the Order of Canada.

GENERAL GEORGES P. VANIER, PC, DSO, MC, CD (1888–1967)

The first French-Canadian governor general since the fall of New France, soldier, diplomat, and consummate statesman, Georges Vanier would become the most beloved representative of the Crown the country has ever known. A hero of the First World War, Vanier and his wife Pauline were inseparable throughout their lives — serving in diplomatic posts in Britain and France. In 1944 he was appointed Canada's first ambassador to France, where he and his wife became renowned for their outreach to countless war refugees. Appointed by the Queen in 1959 to become Canada's governor general, he would undertake an ambitious program until 1966 when health issues began to severely hamper his physical ability. One of the last instruments that Vanier signed was the Order-in-Council authorizing the establishment of the Order of Canada, a project he had taken great interest in throughout his lifetime.

During their meeting, Massey and Matheson discussed problems that might arise with the various possible structures the new order could take. It was soon agreed that the order, as yet unnamed, would have only one level.[35] The single level was agreed to because past governments had rejected multi-level orders on the basis that they encouraged a hierarchy. Upon his return to Ottawa, Matheson reported to the prime minister. That evening, Pearson called on Governor General Georges Vanier to inform him about the project.[36] His Excellency showed strong interest and thought it would be appropriate if his secretary, Esmond Butler, became involved on his behalf. Butler would become key to the order's success. A close friend of Vincent Massey, he, too, was excited by the project: "I would only be too pleased to help in any possible way."[37]

In his report to the prime minister, Matheson noted: "I was delighted with this meeting. My attitudes were solely upon research. Mr. Massey's views were based upon widespread experience."[38] Aware that the creation of a national honour could develop into a contentious issue, he assured Pearson that "Mr. Massey's sense of harmony and aesthetics is such that we can move with far greater assurance on this matter than on the flag."[39]

The scars of the flag debate were only just healing. These developments led the prime minister to create an ad hoc committee charged with overseeing the creation of a Canadian order.[40] This four-member committee, which Pearson referred to as his "honours team," consisted of John Matheson, Esmond Butler, John S. (Jack) Hodgson, and Michael Pitfield. These four began fleshing out Massey's proposals and structuring the Order of Canada.

Jack Hodgson, Pearson's principal secretary, was an unlikely civil servant. He was a distinguished scholar with several academic degrees in music. He rose to the rank of commander during the Second World War and went on to serve in a variety of senior civil service posts. Pitfield was a civil servant in the Privy Council Office. A lawyer by profession, he possessed natural political insight.

After meeting with Matheson, and with Pearson's approval, Massey set about drafting a constitution for the new order. What he developed was a Canadian version of the British Order of Merit: a single-level order consisting of the sovereign, the governor general, and twenty-five members. Massey appears to have put more thought into the design of the insignia than into the mechanics of the order itself. Nevertheless, this was a significant departure from his earlier proposals for a multi-level order with as many as five grades.

Massey completed his proposal on March 28 and posted it to Matheson the following day. The order still had no name, the two men having been unable to agree on one. Matheson immediately went to work defining the mechanics of the order. The single-level honour was to be styled "The Order of Canada" and to consist only of Companions. Recipients would be entitled to use the post-nominal initials OC.

Recipients were to be chosen by an honours committee, which was to be composed of the chief justice of Canada, the Clerk of the Privy Council (as Registrar of the Order), the under-secretary of state, the under-secretary of state for external affairs, and the Chief of Defence Staff. As with all proposals dating back to the 1930s, the prime minister would hold a veto over nominations. Butler arranged a meeting with Matheson and Pitfield on April 5 to review Massey's proposal.[41]

At this meeting it was decided that the idea of a single-level order — so limited in membership — was too elitist and would fail to gain Cabinet approval. The order was broadened to three levels. However, Pitfield and Matheson could not reach agreement on its actual structure, so two separate proposals were drafted: one each from Pitfield and Matheson. Pitfield spent most of a week drafting his memorandum to the prime minister. He took pains to demonstrate the need for a Canadian order, emphasizing that the "Centennial of Confederation now provides as [sic] unique opportunity to escape the handicap that historical development in this area has cast upon it."[42] He noted that failure to act would result in further reliance on semi-official and "frequently artificial honours" from public and private organizations that "can never assume to be national expressions of commendations, gratitude or encouragement."[43]

Pitfield's proposal clearly reflected the recommendations of the Special Committee on Honours and Decorations, as well as the suppressed proposal of the Royal Commission on National Development in the Arts, Letters and Science, 1951. He emphasized the need for a "distinctly Canadian" order. The method of selection was to be made "secure from partisanship or favouritism." The Canadian system "must provide for the recognition of 'ordinary' as well as 'great' people," and it must encourage outstanding service. Finally, Pitfield outlined the precise structure of the order. It was to consist of three levels:

- Companions, limited to fifty Canadians, with no more than five being appointed a year. They would be entitled to the appellation "Honourable" and to the post-nominal initials COC. In addition to this, Companions would receive the Canada Medal (in gold) with jewel and collar.

- Members, limited to twenty-five appointments per year, with a membership limited to three hundred. They would receive the Canada Medal (in silver) and jewel (collar badge), and would be entitled to the post-nominal initials MOC.
- Associates, limited to one hundred awards per year, with no limit on the overall membership. Associates would receive the Canada Medal (in bronze)[44] and be entitled to the post-nominal initials CM.

Appointments would be made by the Queen, on the advice of the governor general and the Committee of Honours and Awards. This committee was to consist of the governor general as Chancellor of the Order, the chief justice of Canada, the Speaker of the House of Commons, the Speaker of the Senate, the chairman of the Canada Council, the president of the Royal Society of Canada, the under-secretary of state, the Clerk of the Privy Council, and the secretary to the governor general.

Pitfield's memorandum was sent to Pearson on April 13, after it was cleared by Matheson. Unhappy with Pitfield's detailed proposal, Matheson attached a four-page cover letter outlining a different proposal. He let Pearson know that Pitfield's proposal "does not harmonize with your views, nor, upon careful reflection and further research, with my own."[45]

Vincent Massey's official photo portrait as Governor General of Canada.

Matheson's augmentations to Pitfield's memorandum were both aesthetic and practical. The three levels were to be styled Companions, Officers, and Members. In a more practical vein, Matheson made changes to the Honours and Awards Committee. Pearson was skeptical of the proposed prime ministerial veto, noting that "this might be an embarrassment sometimes."[46] Overall, however, he found the proposal satisfactory.[47] Pearson favoured Matheson's revisions to Pitfield's proposal. The project was now in the hands of the prime minister.

There was a strong sense among the key players that if the project was to succeed, it would have to be implemented quickly. Butler coaxed Vanier to discuss the matter further with Pearson: "I think it will be most useful if you could ask the PM what the situation is concerning honours and awards. If a decision is not taken very shortly it would seem to me that it would be impossible to implement any plans in time for 1967."[48]

Massey was also fretting about the seeming lack of progress. At Butler's insistence, he wrote Vanier expressing concern about the glacial pace of the proposed order: "If we lose this opportunity of getting something in the field of honours, it will never occur. Do forgive me for writing to you — I am taking advantage of the fact that you and I are old friends and can talk to each other very frankly."[49]

In response to Massey's constant inquiries, unofficial word came from the prime minister. Vanier wrote Massey a personal letter about the project: "This is a matter which the PM and I have discussed on several occasions. I know that he is, as I am, keenly interested and aware of the danger of delay which you point out. *Je crois que nous sommes tous les trois d'accord*; and I am hopeful."[50] This was the first indication from Pearson that the project was in all likelihood going to proceed for the Centennial.

Butler again encouraged Massey to take action and to write directly to the prime minister — an unusual step.[51] Massey wrote Pearson outlining six reasons why Canada should create a national honour. He was, in fact, preaching to the converted. Massey emphasized that honours could help national unity and promote a sense of identity, and they were an excellent means for the state to say "thank you to a citizen for outstanding achievement."[52] Pearson's response was concise and positive: "I am really anxious to proceed … and have taken certain necessary preliminary steps."[53]

The creation of the Canadian order was set to move forward; the first appointments would be announced on Dominion Day in the Centennial Year.

During a friendly meeting with the Queen's private secretary, Sir Michael Adeane, Pearson asked him to mention the Canadian order to Her Majesty.[54] Adeane was very positive, and most pleased that the prime minister had taken the time to discuss the matter with him.

Frequently, opposition from the prime minister or Cabinet had derailed attempts to create a Canadian order. Regardless of how ill planned or well planned a proposal was, it could flourish or be crushed according to the will of Cabinet and the personalities sitting around the council table. The main difference in 1966 was that the prime minister was a strong supporter and carefully consulted on and constructed the proposal.

Cabinet's reaction was on the whole favourable. A confidential memorandum was circulated to Cabinet on November 7, 1966. It outlined the reasons why Canada needed a system of honours and awards, and most specifically a national order. The Order of Canada / L'Ordre du Canada would consist of three grades:

1. Companions: never to exceed thirty persons; ten appointments to be made in the Centennial year, and not more than five in every year thereafter.
2. Officers: never to exceed one hundred persons; twenty-five appointments in the Centennial year, and not more than ten in any year thereafter.
3. Members: fifty appointments in any year.[55]

The remainder of the proposal was identical to the augmentations Matheson had made to Pitfield's memorandum in April of that year. The selection committee had been re-titled Advisory Council. The subject was added to the agenda of the November 29 Cabinet meeting.

In the weeks leading up to the November 29 meeting, opposition was voiced by Paul Martin, Sr. and Paul Hellyer. Both men would be absent from the upcoming meeting, but they made their positions known well before the fateful day. Martin had been against an honours system since Mackenzie King's time. Paul Hellyer was unhappy that there was no separate military division of the Order. It was, after all, Hellyer who had championed the creation of the Centennial Medal, not to mention his department which had been quietly lobbying for a system of honours for the Canadian military for more than twenty years.

When Cabinet met to discuss the matter, Pearson began with a brief synopsis of the history of honours in Canada, emphasizing the symbolic importance that such an institution would have. After reviewing the proposed structure, some members raised questions about the advisability of having different "classes" of honours. There was a fear that Canadians would not look favourably on a system of classed honours of the sort bestowed in European countries. Three voices of opposition were heard: those of Mitchell Sharp, Judy LaMarsh, and Léo Alphonse Joseph Cadieux (associate minister of national defence, representing Hellyer). Sharp and LaMarsh opposed the creation of any order as it was "out of keeping with the egalitarian tradition in Canada."[56] Cadieux merely rearticulated Hellyer's concern about limited military involvement. Other Cabinet members were unhappy that the Advisory Council consisted solely of federal officials, with no provincial input or involvement from beyond the governmental sphere.[57]

A compromise was eventually reached. Fearing that the entire project might be lost, Pearson agreed to sacrifice the three-level order for a very different entity: "The Cabinet agreed in principle that an 'Order of Canada' of a single grade be established for award to Canadian citizens for merit, and that details respecting its conditions be generally along the lines outlined by the prime minister but subject to further consideration by him on some of the points raised in the course of discussion."[58] The single grade was agreed on, a multi-level system being seen as too European and elitist. It was a short-sighted change that would, out of necessity, not last long. At last there was victory: for the first time in Canadian history, Cabinet had agreed to the creation of a Canadian order.

Her Majesty the Queen and her Canadian Ministry, 1967, which approved the establishment of the Order of Canada.

Having received Cabinet's provisional approval, Pearson and his staff were faced with the daunting tasks of arranging for all the legal and logistical aspects of establishing the Order of Canada, well beyond simply drafting the necessary documents to legally create the Order. All of this had to be done in time for Dominion Day 1967 — seven months away. The arrangements were made largely by Pearson's quartet of honours experts, whom he affectionately dubbed his "honours team." Although not an official member of the ad hoc committee, Edythe MacDonald would be responsible for ensuring the legal soundness of the Order's constitution and letters patent.

The Queen, as Canada's head of state, was the only logical choice as Sovereign of the Order, so her permission had to be sought. On January 6, 1967, Butler posted a letter to the Queen's private secretary, Sir Michael Adeane. The letter included a brief summary of the initial proposals and Matheson's October 19 draft constitution for the Order.[59]

Insignia for the Order of Canada and the Seal of the Order as approved by the Queen.

ESMOND U. BUTLER, CVO, OC (1922–1989)

The longest serving secretary to the governor general in Canadian history and the first secretary general of the Order, Esmond Butler was a passionate supporter and developer of the modern Canadian honours system. Having served in the Royal Canadian Naval Volunteer Reserve during the Second World War, Butler spent time in Switzerland with United Press International, and then went on to work as assistant secretary to Vincent Massey, followed by a brief stint as assistant press secretary to the Queen. In 1959 he was appointed secretary to Governor General Georges Vanier, a post he would hold until 1985 when he became Canada's ambassador to Morocco. A man of great dignity and presence, Butler was the institutional memory of Ottawa when it came to not only ceremonies and state events, but also the place of the Crown and role of the governor general in a changing political landscape. He did much to update and modernize the operation of not only Rideau Hall, but the public program of five successive governors general. Butler was appointed an Officer of the Order of Canada in 1986, having previously been made a Commander of the Royal Victorian Order in 1972 in recognition of his service to the Queen and governor general.

On receipt of the letter, Adeane immediately consulted the Queen and sent this telegram to Butler: "The Queen gives provisional approval STOP Letter on its way."[60] In the letter Adeane indicated that the Queen wished "to be consulted about the designs of the … Insignia."[61] Vanier in particular was delighted with news of the approval.[62]

In part to overcome the Cabinet's reluctance to have a multi-level order of Canada established, two clever additions were made to the new institution, although neither returned the Order to its original three levels. The first was the creation of a Medal of Courage of the Order of Canada. This was added in part to address the minister of national defence's concern that the Order was not going to recognize the military. The Medal of Courage of the Order of Canada was to rank after the Victoria Cross and George Cross, but before all other gallantry awards such as the Distinguished Service Cross, Military Cross, and Distinguished Flying Cross.[63] The Medal of Courage was to be "awarded in connection with the Order to any person who, in peace time, as a civilian or a member of an armed force or police force, performs an act of conspicuous courage in circumstances of great danger."[64]

At this point it was assumed that Canada would continue to use the various wartime imperial gallantry decorations — however, by early February this plan was abandoned in favour of an entirely Canadian honours system; the Medal of Courage would serve for all acts of gallantry, military or otherwise, replacing more than ten other gallantry decorations.[65] Approval for the addition of the Medal of Courage was given on January 3, 1967, simultaneously with the request to MacDonald to draft the necessary orders-in-council and letters patent.

The next development further altering the Order came in late February. Esmond Butler met with Gordon Robertson, Clerk of the Privy Council. During their meeting, they agreed that the Order's existing structure would not achieve the prime minister's objectives, notably the recognition of exemplary contributions made at the local or provincial levels. Esmond Butler argued: "By having only one grade to the Order which can only be awarded to relatively few people, it would obviously not be possible to recognize a very broad cross section of the Canadian population. I know that it has always been the prime minister's wish to honour those of more humble station who serve the country in a distinguished way."[66] Robertson suggested that there might also be a "Medal of Service." Pearson accepted this proposal, incrementally getting closer to his goal of a three-tiered order. The Medal of Service of the Order of Canada was to be awarded for "achievement and merit of a high degree, especially to Canada or to humanity at large."[67] The Medal of Service would rank after the Medal of Courage. The Order of Canada now had three honours covering two fields: service and gallantry.

On March 2, the proposal for the Medals of Courage and Service passed through Cabinet without serious incident.[68] Writing on February 27 to Governor General Vanier, Adeane noted the Queen's enthusiasm for the Order and how delighted she was to see Canada create this new institution.[69]

All of the relevant founding documents had by now been drafted by MacDonald. The constitution submitted to the governor general, and later the Queen, founded an order consisting of three components:

- *Companion of the Order of Canada*, to be "made for merit, especially service to Canada or to humanity at large." For the Centennial year, provision was made for fifty people to be appointed, with a maximum of twenty-five in successive years. Membership in this level was limited to 150 Companions in addition to the Sovereign and Chancellor. Recipients would be entitled to the post-nominal initials CC.
- *Medal of Courage of the Order of Canada*, to be awarded to "any person who, as a civilian or a member of an armed force or police force performs an act of conspicuous courage in circumstances of great danger." There was no limit on the number of Medals of Courage that could be awarded. Those who received the Medal of Courage would be entitled to the post-nominal initials CM.
- *Medal of Service of the Order of Canada*, to be awarded "to any person for merit, especially service to Canada or humanity at large." A maximum of one hundred awards would be made during the Centennial year, and fifty in each year thereafter. Recipients would be entitled to the post-nominal initials SM.

ABOVE: Case for the Companion of the Order of Canada insignia.

TOP LEFT AND TOP: Companion of the Order of Canada insignia.

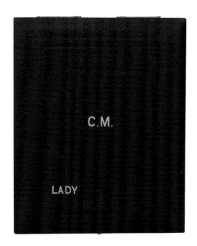

ABOVE: Case for the Medal of Courage of the Order of Canada.

FAR LEFT AND LEFT: Medal of Courage of the Order of Canada.

ABOVE: Case for the Medal of Service of the Order of Canada.

TOP AND TOP RIGHT: Medal of Service of the Order of Canada.

Nominations were to be solicited from the general public. Companions of the Order of Canada and recipients of the Medal of Service of the Order of Canada were to be selected by the Advisory Council of the Order. This council would consist of seven members: the governor general as Chancellor; the chief justice (chairman); the Clerk of the Privy Council; the under-secretary of state; the chairman of the Canada Council; the president of the Royal Society of Canada; and the president of the Association of Universities and Colleges of Canada. In addition to these members, a secretary for the order was appointed. By virtue of his office, the secretary to the governor general was chosen. Provision was made for the governor general to appoint additional council members. Although nominations for the Medal of Courage would be accepted from the public, the Decorations Committee was expected to submit the bulk of the nominations. Ultimately, it was left to the Decorations Committee to decide on awards of the Medal of Courage; that committee would then submit its provisional list to the Advisory Council. In essence, the Advisory Council was to deal with merit and the Decorations Committee with deeds of bravery.

On March 2, the Governor-in-Council passed Order-in-Council 1966-389, authorizing the submission of the letters patent and constitution of the Order of Canada to the Queen. This would be the last order-in-council signed by Vanier. The documents

P. MICHAEL PITFIELD, PC, OC, CVO (1937–)

Born in Montreal, Michael Pitfield attained an undergraduate degree at the age of sixteen and would go on to study law at McGill. In 1959 he joined the federal civil service as a young assistant to Minister of Justice Davie Fulton and would hold a number of other similar appointments in the Privy Council Office, becoming assistant clerk in 1966. Within PCO Pitfield was Pearson's point man on establishing the Order of Canada, and it was he who was charged with fleshing out the details of the Order's structure with Vincent Massey, Esmond Butler, and John Matheson before the proposal was presented to Cabinet. A brilliant administrator, Pitfield succeeded his mentor, Gordon Robertson, as Clerk of the Privy Council in 1975, and would serve in that role until 1979 and again from 1980 to 1982. He was then summoned to the Senate, where he sat as an independent, retiring in 2010. Throughout the constitutional negotiations of the late 1970s and early 1980s, he was a central player. In 1982 he would be appointed a Commander of the Royal Victorian Order in recognition of his work on the Constitution and various matters touching on the role of the Crown and governor general. In 2012, he was appointed an Officer of the Order of Canada. He has long been an outspoken advocate of issues regarding Parkinson's, from which he suffers.

BELOW: Letters Patent establishing the Order of Canada.

LETTERS PATENT

establishing the

ORDER OF CANADA

Effective July 1, 1967

DATED ...... 21st March, 1967
RECORDED ... 18th April, 1967
Film 203 Document 19

DEPUTY REGISTRAR GENERAL OF CANADA

Canada

ELIZABETH THE SECOND, by the Grace of God of the United Kingdom, Canada and Her other Realms and Territories QUEEN, Head of the Commonwealth, Defender of the Faith.

TO ALL TO WHOM these Presents shall come or whom the same may in anywise concern.

GREETING:

WHEREAS it is desirable and Our Privy Council for Canada has advised that Letters Patent do issue establishing a society of honour in Canada to be known as the Order of Canada, for the purpose of according recognition to Canadian citizens and other persons for merit or for courage.

NOW KNOW YE that by and with the advice of Our Privy Council for Canada, We, by these Presents, do institute, erect, constitute and create a society of honour to be known by and have for ever hereafter, the name, style and designation of the "Order of Canada".

AND WE DO ordain, direct and appoint that the said Order shall consist of the Sovereign, the Governor General of Canada and such members together with such honorary members as We, Our heirs and successors or Our Governor General of Canada on Our behalf shall, in accordance with the constitution of the Order, from time to time appoint.

AND WE DO further ordain, direct and appoint that the said Order shall be governed by the Constitution of the Order of Canada set out in the Schedule hereto and by such ancillary Ordinances as may from time to time be established, made, amended and abrogated by Our Governor General of Canada.

travelled from desk to desk, starting with Prime Minister Pearson and moving to Gordon Robertson, Clerk of the Privy Council, then to Judy LaMarsh, secretary of state, on March 13, 1967.[70] Robertson asked LaMarsh to inform him "of the Queen's approval when it has been obtained."[71] From here, the documents were sent on to Esmond Butler and the governor general at Rideau Hall. Unfortunately, on March 5, General Vanier died and the submission had to be made by the administrator of the Government of Canada, Chief Justice Robert Taschereau. Finally, on March 17, the prime minister's submission was forwarded to the Queen.[72] On March 21 the Queen approved and signed the letters patent founding the Order of Canada, to take effect on July 1, 1967.[73]

On April 17, Pearson rose in the House of Commons to announce the establishment of the Order:

> Mr. Speaker, I would like to announce to the house the establishment of a system of honours and awards for Canada. Practically every sovereign country has such a system which it uses as a means of recognizing merit or gallantry, or distinguished public service. I believe that recognition of this kind can strengthen national pride and the appreciation of national service. There has been no system of Canadian honours and awards. The Canada Medal was instituted in 1943 as a possible way of filling the gap, but it has never been awarded and is now being replaced. Because Canada has lacked an official system a number of unofficial and semi-official honours and awards have developed over the years…. It is my pleasure to announce that on the recommendation of the government Her Majesty has approved the issue of letters patent constituting the Order of Canada…. Any person or organization is invited at any time to suggest names of persons whom they consider worthy of receiving any of these awards…. The government believes that these three awards, the Companion of the Order of Canada, the Medal of Courage and the Medal of Service, will help fill a need in our national life and will enable proper recognition to be given by Canada to its own citizens and to others.[74]

The leader of the Opposition, John Diefenbaker, then rose and recounted a brief history of honours in Canada. Although he gave a fairly accurate account, he went on to dissect and criticize Mackenzie King's honours policy and correctly pointed out that Canada had taken such a long time to create a system mainly as result of "Mackenzie King's lengthy period of service as Prime Minister."[75] Diefenbaker offered neither criticism nor support for the endeavour. This was due in part to the fact that he had not been extended the traditional courtesy of being informed beforehand of such an important announcement. This failure to inform the leaders of the opposition parties also accounted for the absence of the NDP leader. David Lewis endorsed the Order on behalf of the NDP: "On behalf of our party … we greet the announcement of a Canadian order and the fact that it is Canadian." Lewis pointed out that thousands of Canadians go unrecognized for the contributions they make to their communities, and that the creation of the Order was a good step. In closing, he applauded the method of selection through the Advisory Council and suggested that "the same attitude and the same process [of fairness] will be applied to a good many other appointments in our society, which I think would do Canada a great deal of good."[76]

News of the Order of Canada was now in the public domain; the hard task of selecting recipients could begin. The most noteworthy aspect of the new Order was the method by which recipients were to be selected. The Advisory Council of the Order of Canada had been given the power — hitherto the prime minister's alone — to advise the sovereign. In effect, a portion of the Royal Prerogative, which had been persistently eroded by successive governments both in Canada and throughout the Commonwealth, had been returned to the Queen. The Advisory Council of the Order of Canada provided the first purely non-partisan method of selecting citizens to receive national honours. The emphasis on the role of the citizenry in the nomination process was indicative of the grassroots local involvement that the Centennial was attempting to promote; in effect, this role made the legal category of Canadian citizenship a living social and cultural experience. At the same time, the Order as an institution fit neatly into another goal of the Centennial, which was to promote an "official understanding of Canada."[77] The new Order was to promote both Canadian unity and citizenship idealism.

ORDER OF CANADA
GOVERNMENT HOUSE
OTTAWA

Dear Sir,

    The Rt. Hon. Lester B. Pearson, Prime Minister of Canada, announced in the House of Commons on April 17 a new, distinctly Canadian system of honours and awards to be known as the Order of Canada. Since that time the Chancellor of the Order, His Excellency the Rt. Hon. Roland Michener, has established at Government House a Secretariat for the Order that will receive confidential nominations for appointments.

    According to the Constitution of the Order any organization or individual may submit to the Secretary General of the Order, for consideration by the Advisory Council, a nomination of a Canadian citizen for appointment to the Order.

    As you may know, the Constitution also provides for the Governor General to appoint, during 1967, up to fifty Companions of the Order and to award as many as one hundred Medals of Service. The appointments made will include only those nominees who have given distinguished service of the very highest order to Canada or to humanity at large.

    The Secretariat is now beginning to prepare a list of nominations for the consideration of the Advisory Council. To ensure the greatest possible public knowledge of the Order, the Secretariat is circulating to some hundreds of national and provincial organizations the enclosed pamphlet describing the Order in more detail. It is hoped that in this way a comprehensive and representative list of nominations, including the names of distinguished Canadians from every field of endeavour in Canadian life, can be placed before the Advisory Council for its consideration.

    If there is some outstanding Canadian whose name you feel should be considered by the Advisory Council, I should be grateful if you would submit a confidential nomination to the Secretary General of the Order, Government House, Ottawa.

Yours sincerely,

Esmond Butler,
Secretary General of the Order of Canada.

Esmond Butler's announcement of the Order's creation.

With the establishment of the Order of Canada on April 17, 1967, and the issuing of Order-in-Council 1967-388, the Canada Medal ceased to be.[78] The creation of the Order under the Pearson government, in such a short period of time, highlights the prime minister's perception that the country needed new Canadian institutions that emphasized the role of citizens and the unity of Canada. Although the Order of Canada was developed at the most senior levels, its emphasis on involving the citizenry through grassroots nominations and on opening the honours system to non-traditional groups, obviously reflected the politics of the 1960s — specifically, the idealism and nationalism aroused by the Centennial.

Following the announcement of the Order of Canada, Cabinet again returned to one of the original questions that had helped spur interest about Canadian honours in the first place: the proposal for a Centennial of Confederation Commemorative Medal. Cabinet, now largely free of its honours phobia, approved the creation of this special commemorative medal, which was to be awarded to 29,500 Canadians who had performed "valuable service to the nation."

BELOW: Press Release announcing the Order of Canada.

ORDER OF CANADA
GOVERNMENT HOUSE
OTTAWA

JULY 6, 1967.

PRESS RELEASE FROM THE SECRETARIAT OF THE
ORDER OF CANADA, GOVERNMENT HOUSE, OTTAWA

The Right Honorable Roland Michener, Chancellor of the Order of Canada, made today the first appointments to membership in the Order of Canada. Thirty-five Canadians were appointed Companions of the Order, and fifty-five Medals of Service were awarded.

By its Constitution, the Order of Canada is deemed to have been instituted on July 1, 1967. Provision is made for the appointment from that date until the end of 1967 of up to fifty Companions of the Order and for the awarding of as many as one hundred Medals of Service. In addition to the appointments made today, it is expected that further appointments, some with special Centennial significance, will be made before the end of the Centennial Year.

The Canadians whose names appear on the two lists for the Companionship and the Medal of Service were appointed by His Excellency the Governor General with the approval of Her Majesty The Queen, who is Sovereign of the Order, and on the

...2

2.

recommendation of the Advisory Council of the Order. The Advisory Council made its selection on the basis of "merit, especially service to Canada or humanity at large", from nominations submitted by a large number of Canadian individuals and organizations.

In its report to the Chancellor, the Advisory Council stated that it had not considered nominations of active party politicians or members of the Advisory Council itself, believing that the eligibility of Canadians in these two categories should be considered after their present activities have been completed.

In expressing its appreciation for the widespread public support evidenced in the large number of nominations it had received, the Advisory Council noted that, although the names of many outstanding Canadians could not be included in a short preliminary list, it was expected that they would appear on future lists. In this connection, the Advisory Council expressed the hope that all persons and organizations wishing to make nominations would do so to ensure that such nominations are certain to be considered. Such nominations should be sent to: The Secretary General, Order of Canada, Government House, Ottawa.

As will be remembered, the Advisory Council consists of the following six members who hold office ex officio:

The Chief Justice of Canada

...3

The first honours list was published in the *Canada Gazette* and released to the public on July 7, 1967. The list included such notables as Dr. Wilder Penfield, Vincent Massey, Madame Pauline Vanier, Major General George Pearkes, M.J. Coldwell, Gaetan Gélinas, Maurice "the Rocket" Richard, and Marlene Streit. In total, thirty-five Companions and fifty-five Medals of Service were appointed that month. A second list of fifteen Companions and forty-five Medals of Service was issued in December 1967. The first member of the Order was Roland Michener, who was invested by the Queen on July 6, 1967, at Government House.

```
                        (Please check against Delivery)

Notes for the Governor General's Remarks at a Joint
Luncheon Meeting of the Kiwanis and Rotary Clubs,
MacDonald Hotel, Edmonton, 7th November, 1967


(Introductory Remarks)


                    Honours in Canada

        Some people might think this a rather obscure
subject to engage their attention but others, who ap-
preciate the recognition of significant service to the
country, will be pleased with the establishment this year
of the Order of Canada.  This act of the Canadian Govern-
ment will take its place among the many events of enduring
importance which have marked our celebration of the
Centennial of Confederation.

        Although Canada is basically a democratic society of
freedom seeking pioneers, it has not been lacking in
nobility.  In fact the earliest settlements in our country
were based on the seigniorial system.  In many ways it was
exactly the same system that had prevailed in France for
centuries.  The first grant of land in New France was made
by Champlain to the Sieur de la Roche in 1598.  The document
outlining the principles of the seigniorial system reads
in part as follows:

        "In order to increase and extend the goodwill, courage
        and affection of those who are about to embark in the
        said undertaking . . . we have given him authority to
        grant . . . full property to . . . gentlemen and . . .
        persons of merit in the form of seigniories, fiefs,
        chatellenies, earldoms, viscounties, baronies and other
        dignities . . . on condition that they shall aid in the
        support and defence of the territories . . ."

        The seigniory system took root and flourished long after
the feudal principles on which it had been founded died
out in Europe, and General Murray was able to describe its
continuing hold on the country when he took command of
the colony in 1760, 162 years later:  "fiefs or seigniories
. . . are deemed noble; on the demise of the possessor,
his eldest son inherits one half and shares with the other
children in the remainder.  The seigniors have the right
of . . . holding courts of various degrees of importance."

                        . . . . . .
```

Roland Michener's first speech on the Order of Canada.

Two weeks prior to the Order's first investiture ceremony, the governor general made the first speech in which he, as Chancellor, made reference to the new Order. "I think you will agree that the Order of Canada represents a worthy and distinctive way in which we may honour Canadians who have earned our continuing respect and recognition…. As I see it, the Governor General represents first our Constitutional Monarchy, which has given stability and continuity to parliamentary democracy over the years, and represents at the same time the Canadian people and their institutions as a whole. It seems to me that the Order of Canada, which honours distinguished service by Canadians from every region and walk of life, should add to our sense of togetherness by giving recognition and honour to those who have served the whole realm."[79]

By that time Michener had himself been invested as the Order's first Companion, and he had endured hearing multiple accounts of the deliberations of the inaugural meeting of the Advisory Council of the Order from Esmond Butler. Throughout his time as governor general, Michener exuded a joyous approach to investiture ceremonies and interacting with the Order's earliest members. There was also a sense of relief that at long last, Canada had finally managed to establish its own national order.

FIVE

THE PATH TO APPOINTMENT

Almost every country in the world has an honours system or official way of
recognizing the exemplary contributions of its citizens. In the context of other
countries, the establishment of a national honour or medal was not a unique
event. Throughout the 1960s, as many of Britain's and France's colonies gained their independence, a colourful array of new orders, decorations, and medals were created. Given
the controversy that surrounded the discontinuation of honours in Canada following
the end of the First World War, it is understandable that the Order of Canada had to
eschew the perception, and reality, that some civil honours bestowed upon Canadians
under the British imperial honours system were patronage and partisan-based rewards.

It was none other than Vincent Massey, the first Canadian-born governor general
since the French Regime, who initially devised the selection process that has played a
significant role in insulating the Order of Canada from the difficulties experienced by
many other honours systems. Massey had a lifelong interest in promoting Canadian
identity, arts, and culture. Following eleven years as Canada's High Commissioner to
the United Kingdom — including the period throughout the Second World War —
Massey was appointed to chair the Royal Commission on the National Development
of the Arts, Letters and Sciences (Massey Commission). The commission included
Arthur Surveyor, founder of the engineering firm SNC Lavelin; Norman Mackenzie,
president of the University of British Columbia; Georges-Henri Lévesque, from the
Université Laval; Hilda Neatby, from the University of Saskatchewan; and Massey, who
at the time was chancellor of the University of Toronto.

R. GORDON ROBERTSON, PC, CC (1917–2013)

Senior adviser to five different prime ministers, Gordon Robertson (pictured with Pierre Trudeau on the left and Ed Schreyer on the right) would serve as Clerk of the Privy Council from 1963 to 1975. Having earned a Rhodes Scholarship, he first went on to serve as assistant to William Lyon Mackenzie King and was subsequently appointed as commissioner of the Northwest Territories. At thirty-six, he remains the youngest person to ever hold the post. A civil servant of immense organizational ability, Robertson did much to guide a succession of prime ministers through the maze that is official Ottawa. Robertson was a long-serving member of the Advisory Council of the Order. Along with Esmond Butler and Michael Pitfield, Robertson was one of the few who was not only involved in the establishment of the Order, but also in its administration and long-term success. Robertson had the original idea behind the Medal of Service of the Order of Canada, which would become the Officer level of the Order in 1972. Appointed a Companion of the Order of Canada in 1976, he spent his retirement advising the federal government and a wide variety of organizations on public policy issues.

Aside from sweeping recommendations for increased support to Canadian arts, culture, universities, and broadcasting, the commission also undertook a detailed study into honours, a topic that came up with regularity as the group travelled Canada seeking submissions and views on all matters touching upon the arts and sciences. The general sentiment was that "this country should have its own orders … and that through them the Dominion might confer fitting distinctions and appropriate honours upon those whom it delighted to honour."[80]

Their final draft report was a comprehensive proposal for the establishment of distinctive Canadian order of chivalry to be known as the Order of St. Lawrence. What was unique about the proposal was that while appointments would be made by the King, they would be made on the recommendation of an arm's length and non-partisan committee to be known as the "Honours Committee" — the prime minister and Cabinet would no longer have a role in selecting recipients. This was a significant departure from the way in which honours recommendations were made in other parts of the world. Sadly for the commission, and in contempt of Parliament, the honours section of the Royal Commission's final report was suppressed by the government of the day. Prime Minister Louis St. Laurent was focused on an impending federal election and also likely harboured concerns about being responsible for the establishment of a new national honour that, by happenstance, bore his own surname — a move that would have certainly precipitated comment from the opposition parties.

When plans to establish the Order of Canada were initiated in 1966, Massey was one of the first people consulted, his longstanding interest in and knowledge of honours and his passion for Canadian symbols being well known. Massey's plan for an honours committee was modified and transformed into an Advisory Council. Chaired by the Chief Justice of the Supreme Court of Canada, the council was also to include the Clerk of the Privy Council, under-secretary of state for Canada, president of the Royal Society of Canada, chairman of the Canada Council, and president of the Association of Universities and Colleges of Canada, with the secretary to the governor general acting as secretary of the council.

The first meeting of the Advisory Council took place at Rideau Hall on June 13, 1967, and lasted two days. Chief Justice Robert Taschereau acted as chair, with Clerk of the Privy Council Gordon Robertson, president of the Royal Society of Canada Jean Martineau, chair of the Canada Council and Nobel Prize-winner Gerhard Herzberg, and president of the Associations of Universities and Colleges Canada Walter H. Johns around the table. Esmond Butler, the secretary to the governor general, was also present, along with the first employee of the Order's secretariat, Joyce Bryant. There was an immediate sense of "feeling one's way around a new institution with the realization that precedent was going to be set."[81] This sentiment was emphasized by Butler in his opening remarks: "My first words must be an appeal for forbearance. Just over one month ago, the prime minister announced the establishment of the Order of Canada. We had no staff, no office space or equipment, no precedents to follow, and a Chancellor only a few hours old. He has aged considerably since then!"[82]

From there the council began the process of wading through hundreds of nominations submitted from across Canada. Over the following years, a formalized process for assessing each nomination was developed. The Advisory Council found the selection of the first Companions to be a relatively easy task. The secretariat then tabulated the names and told the council which names had been unanimously approved. The first five nominees agreed on were Pauline Vanier, Major General George Pearkes, Dr. Wilder Penfield,

A completed Order of Canada nomination form, c. 1967.

July 7, 1967.

Dear Mr. Massey:

  I have been instructed by His Excellency the Rt. Hon. Roland Michener, Chancellor and Principal Companion of the Order of Canada, to inform you of your appointment as Companion of the Order of Canada, which entitles you to use the initials C.C. after your name.

  Plans are being made for an Investiture this fall when you will receive the insignia of the Order. I shall be writing to you again as soon as more details are available.

  Meanwhile, may I, on behalf of the Governor General, extend to you his congratulations and good wishes.

    Yours sincerely,

    Esmond Butler

    Esmond Butler,
    Secretary General.

The Rt. Hon. Vincent Massey,
Batterwood House,
Port Hope, Ontario.

TELEGRAM SENT VIA CNR

      Batterwood House,
       near Port Hope, Ont.

      22nd June, 1967.

Esmond Butler, Esq.,
Secretary General of the Order of Canada,
Government House,
Ottawa, Ont.

THANK YOU FOR MESSAGE. I WOULD BE VERY HAPPY TO

ACCEPT ORDER IF OFFERED

      VINCENT MASSEY

ABOVE: Massey's telegram acceptance of the Order of Canada.

LEFT: Vincent Massey's notification of appointment to the Order of Canada.

BELOW: Vincent Massey shortly after being invested as a Companion of the Order. Massey spent nearly forty years working toward the establishment of a Canadian honour.

Vincent Massey, and Louis St. Laurent. This process was repeated four times until a list of thirty-five had been compiled. The entire list was then reviewed by the Advisory Council. The same process was then repeated for the nominees for the Medal of Service.

  The nomination process has not changed a great deal since 1967, although in addition to submitting a nomination in a written format, an electronic online portal has recently been instituted in an effort to increase the number of annual nominations received by the Chancellery. Various vital statistics are entered into the form, along with details of why the nominee is considered worthy for receiving one of the highest honours of the land. Essentially, nominators are asked to describe why a particular nominee has lived up to the Order's motto, "they desire a better country." Along with the synopsis, nominators include the names of two or three individuals who are willing to support the nomination. From there the nomination is sent in to Rideau Hall where it is processed. In the early years of the Order, upon receipt of nominations from the public, officials at the Order of Canada Secretariat (what is today the Chancellery) took the following eleven steps:

1. A folder is prepared on behalf of the proposed nominee, as well as an index card for record purposes. Biographical material is assembled to document the file for presentation to the Advisory Council.

2. If additional information or supporting data are required, the secretariat may obtain supplementary facts by consulting, in confidence, members of the Order, as well as knowledgeable officials from national and regional organizations, and various other local and provincial sources.

3. The officers of the secretariat assist the Advisory Council by screening nominations, rating them as follows:

   A-level nominees are appropriate for consideration at the Companion and Officer levels.

   B-level nominees are appropriate for consideration at the Member level.

   C (drop) cases are considered not to meet the minimum criteria for appointment.

   D cases require more research.

4. At least one month prior to each semi-annual meeting, a list of A and B level nominees, together with their respective biographical sketches, is completed, compiled, and forwarded to the Advisory Council for consideration.

5. Prior to each meeting, additional confidential assessments are obtained from consultants in various spheres of endeavour as a means to assist the Advisory Council in its deliberations.

6. The Advisory Council meets twice yearly, in April and October, to review nominations previously submitted to each member, as well as a list of special cases tabled at the meeting. In addition to its preliminary work, the

GERHARD HERZBERG, PC, CC (1904–1999)

One of the first members of the Advisory Council of the Order, Gerhard Herzberg was at the time president of the Royal Society of Canada. Born in Hamburg, Germany, Herzberg would take up a guest professorship at the University of Saskatchewan in 1935 as the situation in his native land began to deteriorate with the Nazis consolidating power. He was the world's foremost expert in molecular spectroscopy and did much to expand our knowledge of the electronic structure and geometry of molecules. In recognition of his contributions to science, Herzberg was appointed a Companion of the Order of Canada in 1968 and was subsequently awarded the Nobel Prize for Chemistry in 1971. His gravitas and calm demeanour is said to have played an important part in the early deliberations of the Advisory Council — when processes and methods of selection were being developed.

Esmond Butler 3
SECRETARY TO THE GOVERNOR-GENERAL
CHEF DU CABINET DU GOUVERNEUR GÉNÉRAL

Professor A.R.M. Lower, MA, Ph.D., LL.D., etc.,
Horizon House,
Collins Bay,
Kingston, Ontario.

👑
ORDER OF CANADA
GOVERNMENT HOUSE
OTTAWA

CONFIDENTIAL

November 19, 1968.

Dear Professor Lower

hancellor has asked me
y Council of the Order
name to him for
e Order.

erefore, to ask whether
t such an award if it
ly decision would be
it would be helpful if
r of acceptance with an
, indicating decorations,
recent photograph. It
of appointments will
December.

ted if you would respect

Yours sincerely,

Ryerdel Marsh
for
Esmond Butler,
Secretary General,
Order of Canada.

.D., LL.D., etc.,

👑
ORDER OF CANADA
GOVERNMENT HOUSE
OTTAWA

20th December, 1968.

Dear Professor Lower,

I have been instructed by His Excellency
the Right Hon. Roland Michener, Chancellor and
Principal Companion of the Order of Canada, to
inform you of your appointment as Companion of the
Order of Canada, which entitles you to use the
initials C.C. after your name.

Plans are being made for an Investiture
next spring, when you will receive the insignia
of the Order. I shall be writing to you again as
soon as more details are available.

The Governor General has asked me to
extend to you his warmest congratulations and good
wishes.

Yours sincerely,

Esmond Butler

Esmond Butler,
Secretary General,
Order of Canada.

Professor A.R.M. Lower, CC, MA, Ph.D., LL.D., etc.,
Horizon House,
4205, Bath Road,
Kingston, Ont.

👑
ORDER OF CANADA
GOVERNMENT HOUSE
OTTAWA

28th January, 1969.

Dear Professor Lower,

I have been asked by the Governor General and
Chancellor of the Order of Canada to invite you to an
Investiture of the Order, to be held at Government House
on Tuesday, April 8th, 1969 at 6.00 p.m.

The ceremony will be followed by a reception
and a dinner. The dress for this occasion will be white
tie and decorations, long evening dress for ladies and
mess dress for members of the Armed Forces.

The Chancellor is pleased to inform you that
the Order is authorized to pay the transportation expenses
of each recipient of an award and one guest, to those who
wish to avail themselves of such assistance. (Because of
limitations of space, it is not possible to allow more
than one guest at the Investiture, reception and dinner).
The Registrar of the Order will be happy to arrange
accommodation in Ottawa for those desiring it. The attached
information sheets give more details on these points, and
it would be appreciated if you would complete the enclosed
questionnaire and return it at your earliest convenience.

The Chancellor very much hopes that it will be
possible for you to come to Ottawa for this ceremony and
to receive your award.

Yours sincerely,

Esmond Butler
Esmond Butler,
Secretary General,
Order of Canada.

Professor Arthur R. M. Lower, CC, MA, Ph.D., LL.D., etc.,
"Horizon House",
4205 Bath Road,
Kingston, Ontario.

Various ephemera related to Arthur Lower's appointment as a
Companion of the Order of Canada.

council studies each individual case. After careful consideration, a short list
of A and B level nominees is tabled, from which the names of proposed
appointees are selected for recommendation to the governor general,
Chancellor of the Order. The Chief Justice, as chair of the council, submits
to the Chancellor a letter outlining the council's recommendations.

7. If the Chancellor agrees with the recommendations made by the Advisory
    Council, he (she) submits a list of proposed appointees for approval by Her
    Majesty the Queen, Sovereign of the Order.

ROBERT TASCHEREAU, PC, CC (1896–1970)

A highly respected Canadian jurist and long-time member of the Supreme Court of Canada, Robert Taschereau had previously enjoyed a brief political career as a member of Quebec's House of Assembly from 1930 to 1935 before returning to legal practice. Appointed to the Supreme Court in 1940, he briefly served as chief justice from 1963 to 1967. Taschereau was one of the members of the Royal Commission on Spying Activities that had been established following the Gouzenko Affair, which exposed the existence of a Soviet spy ring in Canada. Taschereau helped to establish the consensus model that the Advisory Council used to select members of the Order until 2000 when a system of voting was instituted. In recognition of his contributions to Canada and the Supreme Court, he was made a Companion of the Order of Canada in December 1967.

8. Following approval of the list by the Sovereign, an Instrument is drawn up, sealed, and signed by the governor general.

9. A preliminary letter is sent to the proposed appointees (or a telephone call is made), seeking their acceptance and asking them to provide an up-to-date biographical sketch and photograph.

10. Biographical material in French and English, as well as prints of the photographs, are compiled by the secretariat for distribution to the press at the time public announcement is made.

11. Prior to the press release, an official letter signed by the Secretary General is sent to recipients, confirming their appointment to the Order and advising them of the forthcoming publication to be made in the *Canada Gazette*. Recipients are also informed that in due course, they will be invited to a ceremony at Rideau Hall or La Citadelle in Quebec City, at which time they will be invested with the insignia of the Order.[83]

As the Order has grown in size and membership, and the number of annual nominations has increased, the membership of the council has also grown to better reflect the diversity of region and achievement that today embodies the Order. The council currently includes the chief justice of the Supreme Court of Canada (chair), Clerk of the Privy Council, deputy minister of Canadian heritage, chairperson of the Canada Council,

Professor Arthur Lower's miniature medal group. Lower would regularly be consulted for advice regarding potential recipients of the Order.

president of the Royal Society of Canada, chairperson of the board of Universities Canada, along with seven additional members drawn from the non-medical sciences, protective services, or the charitable or religious sector.

With more than six hundred nominations received annually, the Advisory Council meets twice a year to review the nominations for appointment and promotion. Nomination packages considered by the Advisory Council have moved from large three-ring binders to an iPad that is loaded with the relevant information for consideration.

SIX

THE FIRST INVESTITURE
AND DINNER

The first investiture held for the Order took place at Rideau Hall during Queen Elizabeth II's 1967 Royal Tour of the country throughout the last part of June and into early July of the momentous centennial year. It was a small affair involving the Queen, Duke of Edinburgh, Governor General and Mrs. Michener, Prime Minister Pearson and his wife Maryon, along with Esmond Butler, the secretary to the governor general, and several other officials from the governor general's household.

At 7:30 p.m. on Wednesday, July 5, 1967, Butler escorted Her Majesty and His Royal Highness into the governor general's study. Once everyone was assembled in the room, Prime Minister Pearson asked Her Majesty to invest the governor general as Chancellor and Principal Companion of the Order. Esmond Butler took in his hands a velvet cushion bearing the first Order of Canada insignia on it and approached the Queen. Her Majesty took the insignia off the cushion and presented it to the governor general. Photographs were then taken, and Her Majesty and Mr. Michener spoke about the importance of what had transpired. The entire ceremony lasted only five minutes, and with that, the first member of the Order was invested. Throughout the remainder of the 1967 Royal Tour, Michener would wear his Companion's insignia on several occasions.

Event plan for the first Order of Canada presentation, July 5, 1967.

Her Majesty the Queen and Roland
Michener at the end of the 1967
Royal Tour. That was the first
occasion when the Order of Canada
insignia was worn in public.

One day after Michener's investiture, at 6:00 p.m. on Thursday, July 6, the first Order of Canada honours list was released to the press for publication the following day. This list contained the names of ninety Canadians. With the announcement made and the Order's membership established, the next task was to arrange for an investiture and dinner to properly honour each of the first Companions and recipients of the Medal of Service.

The first investiture was held on Friday, November 24, 1967, at Rideau Hall in Ottawa. In many ways it was the crowning touch to the Centennial celebrations that had opened the year with the lighting of the Centennial flame in front of Parliament on New Year's Eve. The gathering of nearly ninety eminent Canadians who had all contributed in varying ways to the nation's life and well-being signalled the beginning of the Order of Canada as a fellowship of honour and service. The simplicity of the ceremony did nothing to diminish it; it was a truly Canadian occasion. The affair was formal throughout. The men wore white tie, and the women wore evening dresses. Investees and their spouses were billeted at Ottawa's Skyline Hotel. The ceremony was presided over by the governor general on behalf of the Queen; the dinner was hosted by the acting prime minister, Mitchell Sharp, on behalf of the Government of Canada.

Canada Gazette entry publishing
the first appointments to the
Order of Canada.

ROLAND MICHENER, PC, CC, CMM, OONT, CD, QC (1900–1991)

The first Chancellor of the Order, Roland Michener was a popular governor general who served during a time when there were increasing questions about the role of the Crown and utility of the vice-regal office. Michener did much to articulate the importance of honours and recognizing the great achievements of Canadians from all walks of life. A lawyer by training, Michener was first elected to the House of Commons in 1953, eventually becoming Speaker in 1957, where he served until 1962, when he lost his seat in the House of Commons. In 1963, he was appointed Canada's High Commissioner to India, where he served until 1967, when he was appointed governor general following the untimely death of General Georges Vanier. Along with his wife, Norah, Michener undertook a breakneck pace of Expo 67 and centennial year engagements. Michener became the first Member of the Order of Canada, invested by the Queen at Rideau Hall in July 1967. Throughout his time as governor general, Michener was a strong proponent of physical fitness and a better understanding of the Crown's role. He would also represent Canada abroad on a number of occasions. One of Canada's longest-serving governors general, he made an indelible impression on the office.

Printed program from the inaugural Order of Canada investiture.

VIPs at investiture at Rideau Hall: Mrs. Michener, Mrs. Vanier,
G-G Michener, Mr. Massey, Mr. St. Laurent

90 Canadians honored

By the Canadian Press

With cabinet ministers and their own friends watching on, 35 Canadians Friday were invested as companions in the Order of Canada.

Another 55 received the Order's Medal of Service in an investiture presided over by Governor-General Michener in the sumptuous ballroom of Rideau Hall, the Governor-General's official residence.

Medals of the order rank next only to the Victoria Cross and the George Cross as symbols of devotion to country and humanity.

Mr. Michener, Chancellor of the Order, said all 90 honored Friday "have served their country and their fellows with singular accomplishment and they deserve a full measure of recognition from Canada and its people."

Among those invested as companions of the Order were Vincent Massey, first Canadian-born Governor-General; Montreal Mayor Jean Drapeau; Gen. E. L. M. Burns, Canada's disarmament negotiator at Geneva; former prime minister Louis St. Laurent; novelists Hugh MacLennan and Gabrielle Roy; Mme Vanier, wife of the late Governor-General Vanier; and Dr. Gordon Murray, pioneer in a new operating technique that promises hope for the world's paraplegics.

Those receiving Medals of Service included former Montreal hockey great Maurice "Rocket" Richard, Eskimo carver Kenojuak of Cape Dorset, N.W.T., diplomat Chester Ronning and L. H. Nicholson, former RCMP commissioner.

Creation of the Order was announced in April by Prime Minister Pearson. He said then that Canada must avoid titles, yet reward citizens for great merit and service.

Non-partisan choice

To ensure a non-partisan selection of those honored, an advisory council to consider nominations was composed consisting of the Chief Justice of Canada, the clerk of the privy council, the under-secretary of state, the chairman of the Canada Council, the president of the Royal Society of Canada, and the president of the Association of Universities and Colleges of Canada.

The Order confers no titles or special privileges and has three tiers — Companions of the Order, Medals of Service, and Medals of Courage.

All three medals bear the motto Desiderantes Meliorem Patriam, Latin taken from Hebrews 11.16 and meaning "They desire a better country."

Article from the *Ottawa Journal* about the first investiture.

Recipients arrived at Rideau Hall by 5:00 p.m., and each investee and guest was given a cream-coloured program embossed with the insignia of the Order.

The program listed, in alphabetical order, the names of the first thirty-five Companions and fifty-five recipients of the Medal of Service. Recipients were ushered away to be briefed on how the investiture would unfold. At 5:25 p.m., the recipients were escorted to their assigned places in the ballroom. This was followed by the entrance of the governor general and his consort. The ceremony was officially opened by Roland Michener, Chancellor of the Order. Each Companion's name was read; the recipient then approached His Excellency and was presented with the insignia of Companion of the Order of Canada. They were then directed to a signing table where the Register of the Order was placed, ready for each new member of the Order to inscribe their signature. All of this was repeated with the Medal of Service recipients.

Once all of the recipients had been presented with their insignia or medal, Michener gave a brief address on the significance of the occasion: "All Canadians feel a sense of participation in your achievements. We do not envy your recognition; we envy your attainments. You have been recognized but you are not elevated above us. You personify the ideals of Canada and yet you remain one of us in the strong democratic traditions of this country … the distinguished gathering assembled here tonight truly represents the richness and the vast potential which are offered by our linguistic and cultural duality. It is a richness, it is a potential which has not been fully developed."

Following Michener's speech, "O Canada" was sung and Their Excellencies withdrew from the ballroom. Guests were then invited to attend a reception in the Tent Room before the formal dinner. Following the reception, recipients and guests were taken to the Confederation Room in the West Block of Parliament via bus. The great and the good of the land boarded a pair of large silver buses which were chartered for the occasion.

Sadly, Lester Pearson was unable to attend either the investiture or dinner; he was on an official visit to the United Kingdom. The acting prime minister, Mitchell Sharp, presided over the dinner on his behalf. Sharp was unsure how best to get the assemblage to take their seats; he was rescued by Father Georges-Henri Lévesque, who said grace. It must have been a bitter-sweet moment for Lévesque, who, along with Massey, had worked so diligently as part of the Royal Commission on the National Development of the Arts, Letters and Sciences, which had initially proposed the establishment of a new national honour with a non-partisan selection process. Ironically, two other gentlemen in the room — the former prime minister, Louis St. Laurent, and his Clerk of the Privy Council, Norman A. Robertson — were responsible for the suppression of the Massey Commission's recommendation for the creation of an Order of Canada in 1951! The history of the Order has more than a few instances of those opposing honours gleefully accepting the accolade when offered it. Sharp had at first been opposed to the creation of the Order; however, his views were completely transformed as a result of this first ceremony. He would later write: "It was a brilliant occasion…. Before us was as distinguished a group of Canadians as had ever been assembled in one place."[84]

The dinner began at 8:00 p.m., and consisted of melon prosciutto, *consommé double au sherry*, *filet de boeuf-bouquetière*, and *pommes parisiennes*, followed by *bavaroise à l'ananas*, *petits fours*, *café*, and *vins*. At the head table sat Madame Vanier, John Diefenbaker, Louis St. Laurent, Vincent Massey, M.J. Coldwell, Robert Stanfield, the governor general and Mrs. Michener, and others ranked in the table of precedence. Among the newly appointed Companions one is strained to find an unrecognizable name. Every recipient had contributed to the progress of Canada and the life of its people. The list of Medal of Service recipients was equally outstanding.

The governor general gave the toast to the Queen, as per custom. After the liqueurs, Sharp said a few words about the

Dinner given by the Government of Canada in honour of the Recipients of the Awards of the ORDER OF CANADA

Dîner offert par le Gouvernement du Canada en l'honneur des récipiendaires des décorations de L'ORDRE DU CANADA

Confederation Room
West Block—Parliament Buildings
Friday, 24th November
1967

Salle de la Confédération
Édifice de l'Ouest, Édifices du Parlement
le vendredi 24 novembre
1967

LEFT: Inaugural investiture dinner program.

BELOW: Inaugural investiture dinner seating plan.

Miss Joyce Turpin   SEAT No. 39

DINNER	DÎNER
GIVEN BY	OFFERT PAR
THE GOVERNMENT OF CANADA	LE GOUVERNEMENT DU CANADA
IN HONOUR OF	EN L'HONNEUR DES
THE RECIPIENTS OF THE AWARDS OF THE ORDER OF CANADA	RÉCIPIENDAIRES DES DÉCORATIONS DE L'ORDRE DU CANADA
AT	À LA
CONFEDERATION ROOM WEST BLOCK OTTAWA	SALLE DE LA CONFÉDÉRATION ÉDIFICE DE L'OUEST À OTTAWA
FRIDAY, NOVEMBER 24, 1967	LE VENDREDI 24 NOVEMBRE 1967

The Chancellor and Principal Companion of the Order of Canada

Service

Le Chancelier et Compagnon principal de l'Ordre du Canada

ᵀᵒ à Lieutenant-Colonel the Honourable Henry P. MacKeen, C.D.,Q.C.

Greeting: Salut:

Whereas, with the approval of Her Majesty Queen Elizabeth the Second, Sovereign of the Order of Canada, We have been pleased to award to you the Medal of Service of the Order of Canada

We do by these Presents award you the Medal of Service of the said Order and authorize you to hold and enjoy the dignity of such award together with membership in the said Order and all privileges thereunto appertaining

Given at Rideau Hall in the City of Ottawa under the Seal of the Order of Canada this nineteenth day of December 1969

By the Chancellor's Command,

Roland Michener

Attendu que, avec l'assentiment de Sa Majesté la Reine Elizabeth Deux, Souveraine de l'Ordre du Canada, il Nous a plu de vous décerner la Médaille pour services éminents de l'Ordre du Canada

Nous vous décernons par les présentes la Médaille pour services éminents dudit Ordre et Nous vous autorisons à bénéficier et à jouir de la dignité de cet honneur ainsi que du titre de membre dudit Ordre et de tous les privilèges y afférents

Fait à Rideau Hall, dans la ville d'Ottawa, sous le Sceau de l'Ordre du Canada, ce dix-neuvième jour de décembre 1969

Par ordre du Chancelier,

Le Secrétaire général de l'Ordre du Canada

Esmond Butler

Secretary General of the Order of Canada

RIGHT: Appointment Scroll for the Medal of Service of the Order of Canada.

BELOW: Cover of the first Order of Canada publication.

The Order of Canada

GOVERNMENT HOUSE
OTTAWA

new Order and the assembled recipients. According to Michener, Sharp's speech "gave the occasion the significance which we all hoped for."[85] His brief words "gave a great lift to all who had received the honour and to the standing of the Order itself."[86]

Michener recalled that the investiture ceremony and dinner "satisfied the highest expectations of the most knowledgeable and fastidious. It was quite impressive and even stirring."[87] The first major occasion had been a success; even the most skeptical found words to praise the new Order. By design or by accident, the understated ceremony had captured Pearson's vision. It had counterbalanced the elitism traditionally associated with awards from the state.

SEVEN

EXPANSION AND EVOLUTION: REFORM AND THE BIRTH OF THE CHANCELLERY

Almost immediately after the first letters of appointment were sent out to the new members of the Order of Canada there were problems. Some of those awarded the Medal of Service of the Order of Canada felt they were being given a second-place prize in relation to those appointed as Companions. Part of the reason for this was the insignia presented to Companions as compared to that given to recipients of the Medal of Service. The Companion's insignia was an elegant 18-carat gold white enamel snowflake with a red maple leaf in the centre, surmounted by the Royal Crown that was set with small jewels. The Medal of Service, while attractive, was small and austere by comparison; one-third the size of the Companion's insignia, and struck in sterling silver, the modest silver snowflake looked more like a military decoration than a high civil honour. The belief that the Medal of Service was a consolation prize was highlighted by novelist Morley Callaghan, who refused to accept the Medal of Service of the Order in 1967. Callaghan noted that his colleagues Hugh MacLennan and F.R. Scott had both been appointed Companions, and he could not possibly accept a lesser honour as it would reflect poorly on the calibre of his literary work. It would take fifteen years, but Callaghan would eventually be appointed a Companion of the Order.

Companion of the Order of Canada insignia, second type.

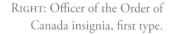

ABOVE: Cases for the Officer of the Order of Canada insignia.

RIGHT: Officer of the Order of Canada insignia, first type.

Prime Minister Pearson had originally intended that the Order of Canada would consist of three levels: Companion, Officer, and Member; however, he was thwarted by a number of Cabinet colleagues — ironically all of whom would go on to be appointed to the Order — who thought that there should not be any levels to the Order. By 1968 the Advisory Council of the Order of Canada decided that the Order should be restructured into three levels: Companion, Officer, and Member — the same arrangement that had been proposed in 1966. This time, however, there was little difficulty in securing acceptance around the table. Those who received the Medal of Service were automatically made Officers of the Order of Canada and invited to exchange their SM insignia for an Officer's insignia — a badge only slightly smaller than that of a Companion and almost as stunning. With this change, the Medal of Service was cancelled.

The scope of achievement required for appointment to each of the three new levels was also more precisely defined. Companions were to be appointed "in recognition of their outstanding achievement and merit of the highest degree, especially in service to Canada or to humanity at large;" Officers were appointed in recognition of "achievement and merit of a high degree, especially service to Canada or to humanity at large;" while Members were appointed for "distinguished service in or to a particular locality, group or field of activity." These changes came into place in 1972 along with the significant expansion of the Canadian honours system.

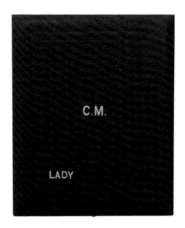

Member of the Order of Canada
cases, lady and gentleman issues.

Member of the Order of Canada,
first type.

In typical Canadian fashion, an interdepartmental committee, called the Working Group on Honours, was struck to advise the prime minister on the changes required to bring about the creation of a fully Canadian honours system. The working group included some of the same people who had overseen the establishment of the Order of Canada, notably Esmond Butler and Michael Pitfield, along with other officials such as

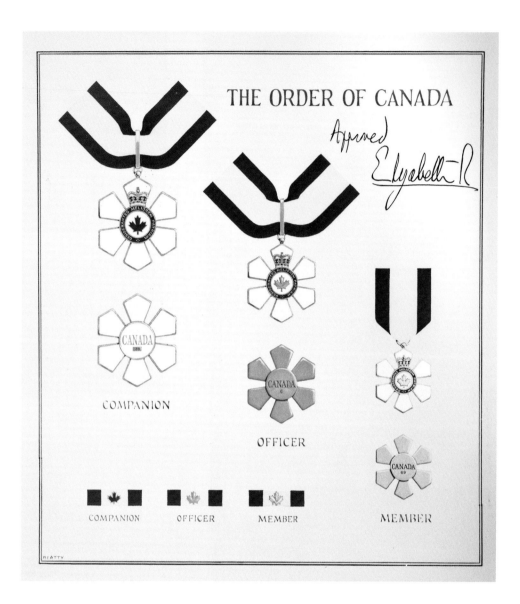

THE ORDER OF CANADA

Approved

Elizabeth R

COMPANION

OFFICER

COMPANION   OFFICER   MEMBER

MEMBER

The Queen's approval for the restructured Order of Canada, 1972.

Carl Lochnan and Roger de C. Nantel. The working group spent several years developing proposals for a multi-faceted Canadian honours system and other more detailed questions related to the administration of honours and foreign honours. The development of military honours, honours for bravery, military service, and, eventually, long service in the various protective services would all be considered by the group.

There was the question of what to do with the Medal of Courage of the Order of Canada — a decoration that was never awarded. The criteria for this award were so broad that it was found impossible to have a single bravery decoration to cover all the varying degrees of courageous acts. Under the imperial honours system, bravery had been divided into four degrees of significance, with the George Cross at the top for the most extraordinary acts of bravery, followed by the George Medal, the Order of the British Empire for gallantry, and the Queen's Commendation for Brave Conduct. So dysfunctional was the concept of a single bravery decoration, that it was decided to continue to use

One of the first Officers of the Order of Canada, pianist Oscar Peterson (left), shortly after being invested, 1973. He was made a Companion in 1984.

appointments to the Order of the British Empire for gallantry into 1968. The Canadian Armed Forces, too, felt as though they were not receiving their share of appointments to the Order of Canada — with military appointments almost entirely going to retired generals and flag officers. Many of the issues that Pearson and his advisers had predicted would befall the new honours on account of Cabinet's meddling came to fruition.

Within a short period of time after the first appointments were made to the Order of Canada, "it was decided … that the Medal of Courage which was incorporated into the Order of Canada would not allow sufficiently for the recognition of acts of bravery."[88] A variety of solutions were considered; however, agreement was reached early on that recognition of brave acts should be done with a separate set of decorations and not the Order of Canada. It was agreed instead that "the Order of Canada should be persuaded to leave the field of bravery awards."[89] To this end, the working group prepared a proposal for three separate bravery decorations: a Hero's Cross, a Medal of Courage, and a Canadian Life-Saving Medal. All would be separate from the Order of Canada.[90] This proposal for three separate decorations emerged in October 1968, and over the next three years were refined into the Cross of Valour, Star of Courage, and Medal of Bravery, although the exact names of each award were not devised until late 1971. The Cross of Valour is awarded for acts of the most conspicuous courage in circumstances of extreme peril, the Star of Courage for acts of conspicuous courage in circumstances of great peril, and, lastly, the Medal of Bravery is conferred in recognition of acts of bravery in hazardous circumstances.

Along with questions related to recognizing brave acts, the working group considered the need to recognize military service, and from this developed the Order of Military Merit — the Order of Canada's military equivalent.

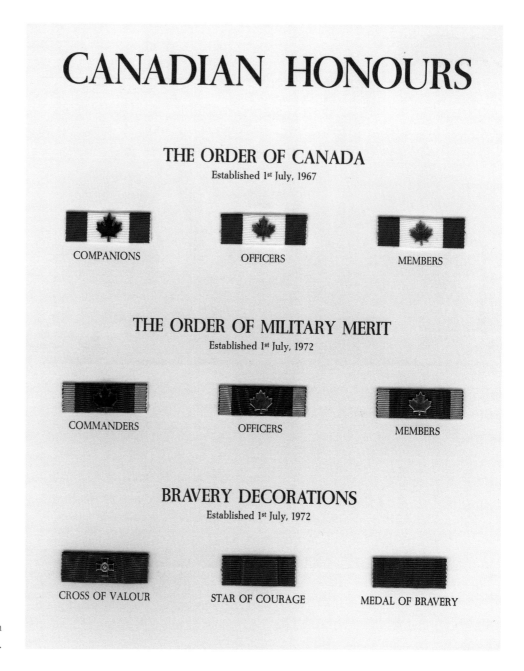

CANADIAN HONOURS

THE ORDER OF CANADA
Established 1st July, 1967

COMPANIONS

OFFICERS

MEMBERS

THE ORDER OF MILITARY MERIT
Established 1st July, 1972

COMMANDERS

OFFICERS

MEMBERS

BRAVERY DECORATIONS
Established 1st July, 1972

CROSS OF VALOUR

STAR OF COURAGE

MEDAL OF BRAVERY

Ribbons of the expanded Canadian honours system in 1972.

It is difficult to believe that, for nearly thirty years, between the end of the Second World War and the establishment of the Order of Military Merit in 1972, members of the Canadian Armed Forces were not eligible for any honours or awards other than for bravery or long service. As we have seen, this vacuum of honours for meritorious military service was one of the catalysts that prompted the creation of the Order of Canada, and the role of the Canadian Armed Forces in pushing for a uniquely Canadian honours system should not be underestimated.

With the foundation of the Order of Canada in 1967, one would assume that the military's desire for a system of honours and awards had been met. This was, however, not the case, and it was determined very early on in the life of the Order of Canada that it

EDYTHE MACDONALD, QC (1931–2009)

One of the few women, aside from the Queen and Joyce Bryant, who was involved in the establishment of the Order of Canada, Edythe MacDonald was a trailblazing pioneer in the male-dominated, stuffy world of official Ottawa in the 1960s. A native of Winnipeg, MacDonald was one of the few women to join the Federal Department of Justice in the late 1950s. There she worked on important legislation, notably changes to the Divorce Act, the Canadian Grains Act, and later the Constitution Act, 1982. MacDonald was responsible for drafting the letters patent and the constitution of the Order of Canada. In 1982 she was appointed to the Ontario Court of Queen's Bench, where she would preside for more than twenty years as a circuit court judge.

Commander of the Order of Military Merit.

LEFT: Officer of the Order of Military Merit.

RIGHT: Member of the Order of Military Merit.

was not a suitable mechanism for the recognition of meritorious service in the Canadian Armed Forces. Early proposals for an order of Canada, dating back to 1944, suggested that it include civilian and military divisions, a concept that was derived from two of the main imperial orders of chivalry — the Order of the Bath and the Order of the British Empire. These recommendations were not followed. In 1966 the Department of National Defence had developed proposals for a Forces Meritorious Cross and a Forces Meritorious Medal, but these plans were shelved in favour of the Order of Canada, which was viewed as the best solution to the absence of a system of military exemplary service awards. The general feeling within DND was that it would therefore be used to recognize both civil and military achievements, in a fashion similar to France's Légion d'honneur (Legion of Honour). As it turned out, the Order of Canada was being conferred almost exclusively as a civilian honour.

Governor General Roland Michener (second from left) and some newly invested Members of the Order of Military Merit.

To ensure that members of the Canadian Armed Forces would be suitably recognized for their meritorious service, the Order of Military Merit was created. Modelled in large part on the restructured Order of Canada, consisting of three levels — Commander, Officer, and Member — appointments to the Order were made on the advice of an advisory committee that would receive nominations from the various elements of the military chain of command. Like the Order of Canada, there was to be no political involvement in any aspect of the Order's nomination process. In 2000 the Order of Military Merit model would be emulated with the establishment of the Order of Merit of the Police Forces, which, as the name suggests, is used to recognize meritorious service over an extended period of time in one of the various police services across Canada.

Another significant change was to further insulate the Order of Canada and the Canadian honours system from the potential of political interference. This was achieved by moving honours administration from the Department of the Secretary of State, from which all civil honours in Canada had been administered since Confederation, to the Office of the Secretary to the governor general. The Honours Secretariat was established, and would eventually grow into what we know today as the Chancellery of Honours.

From the restructuring of the Order of Canada, establishment of the Order of Military Merit, and Canadian Decorations for Bravery has grown an extensive national honours system. The adoption of Pearson's original three-level Order of Canada and the suite of other changes that did much to expand the overall Canadian honours system went through Cabinet without any significant debate. Prime Minister Pierre Trudeau took a more forceful approach to Cabinet's consideration of such symbolic matters. Also in 1972 Canadians resumed being eligible for the non-titular levels of the Royal Victorian Order,

Cross of Valour.

LEFT: Star of Courage.

RIGHT: Medal of Bravery.

which recognizes personal services to the Crown. In the 1980s the family of Exemplary Service Medals were developed, which are awarded for long service in the police, corrections, fire, coast guard, emergency medical, and peace officer services. All of these were based on the two oldest elements of the Canadian honours system: the Royal Canadian Mounted Police Long Service Medal, which had been established by George V in 1934, and the Canadian Forces' Decoration, which dates from 1949 and is awarded to members of the Canadian Armed Forces for long service and good conduct. By 1993 the Military Valour Decorations were created to recognize outstanding valour by those serving in Canada's military. With this the Victoria Cross returned to being Canada's highest honour for military valour, and two new decorations — the Star of Military Valour and Medal of Military Valour — were created by the Queen. These last two decorations were extensively conferred for military valour in Afghanistan. Other important honours, such as the Meritorious Service Cross and Meritorious Service Medal, were also created along with commemorative medals to celebrate the Queen's Silver, Golden, and Diamond jubilees, as well as the Centennial and 125th anniversary of Confederation, and a host of overseas service medals for military service rendered in many different parts of the globe where Canadians are sent as part of coalition, NATO, and United Nations missions. The ten provinces also gradually established provincial Orders, in part modelled on the Order of Canada, during the period between 1979 and 2001.

The restructured Order of Canada came into being in 1972. Since that time there have been few structural changes, aside from enlargements and an alteration in the mechanism through which honorary members are appointed.

ENLARGEMENTS AND CHANGES TO THE ORDER OF CANADA, 1967–2017

Year	Companion	Officer	Member
1967	50 annual (150 max.)	100 (Medal of Service)	None
1972	15 annual (150 max.)	40	80 (new level)
1983	15 annual (150 max.)	46	92
1994	15 annual (150 max.)	50	100
1995	15 annual (165 max.)	50	100
1997	Change in policy toward honorary appointments		
1998	15 annual (165 max.)	52	106
1999	15 annual (165 max.)	64	136
2000	Expansion of the Advisory Council by five members		
2013	Addition of the extraordinary division of the Order		

When the Order was established in 1967, it consisted of two divisions of membership — the general division, which was for all Canadian citizens, and an honorary division, which was intended for non-citizens.

Although the Order's 1967 constitution provided for non-Canadian citizens to be appointed as honorary members of the Order, the enormity of creating an honours system, along with political and bureaucratic delay, prevented any honorary appointments for many years. The first honorary nomination was received in support of Lord Alexander of Tunis in 1967. Alexander, it will be remembered, had served as Canada's governor general from 1946 to 1952, was one of the greatest generals of the Second World War, and had been a highly successful representative of the King during his six years in Canada. It was also Alexander who had pushed Prime Minister Mackenzie King to establish an Order of Canada in 1948. Alas, the government was not willing to move on the appointment of honorary members of the Order, preferring to study the situation further. The next honorary appointment that was nearly made was to John Grierson, film commissioner of the National Film Board during the Second World War and a pioneer in Canadian film. Although he had devoted his life to the arts in Canada, Grierson had never taken Canadian citizenship. His nomination was processed and set forward for approval. Unfortunately, he died the day before it was formally sanctioned — thus no appointment could be made.

It was only after considerable public outcry and numerous articles in the press that the first honorary appointment was made. Zena Sheardown, along with her husband and other members of the Canadian Embassy's staff in Tehran, sheltered six Americans during the Islamic revolution in Iran in 1979. Mrs. Sheardown's role was particularly central since four of the six "houseguests" were billeted with her. She was also at the greatest risk, as she was not a Canadian citizen and was therefore not covered by diplomatic immunity. While the other Canadians who were prominently involved in the sheltering and escape of the six Americans were appointed to the Order on July 1, 1980, there were two prominent omissions. Patricia Taylor, the wife of Canadian ambassador Ken Taylor, and Zena Sheardown, the wife of Canadian diplomat John Sheardown, were both omitted from the list. Immediately after the appointments were announced, there were pointed questions about why these two women had been left unrecognized. The secretary of state for external affairs who was in office at the time of the Tehran incident, Flora MacDonald, took the unprecedented step of introducing a motion on the floor of the House of Commons strongly supporting the nomination of both for the Order. The initial omission was undoubtedly in part the result of gender-bias, along with the problem of Zena Sheardown's lack of Canadian citizenship. Up to that point, no non-Canadian citizen had been appointed to the Order; it would seem the government and the Advisory Council of the Order were still studying the issue more than a decade after it was first raised. Finally, in 1981, Taylor and Sheardown were appointed Members of the Order. With this, Zena Sheardown became the first honorary Member of the Order of Canada; when she later became a Canadian citizen, her honorary membership was cancelled and she was simultaneously appointed a Member of the Order of Canada, general division.

The honorary division of the Order was restructured in 1997 to allow for the appointment of honorary Officers of the Order of Canada, but strangely not Members or Companions. Finally, after more bureaucratic delay and obfuscation, a more refined and complete process for honorary appointments was adopted in 1998.

In September 1998 Nelson Mandela was appointed as the first honorary Companion. This was in recognition of his perseverance through decades of incarceration and his eventual triumph over oppression. Although his achievements were not undertaken in Canada, it was an appropriate honour, being that Canada was one of the first countries to condemn apartheid and to impose sanctions on the regime that Mandela had devoted his life to removing. In August 2001, on her one hundredth birthday, Queen Elizabeth the Queen Mother was appointed the first female honorary Companion of the Order. She had been proposed for nomination as an honorary Companion in 1967 and over the ensuing four decades more nominations were submitted in favour of her appointment.

Zena Sheardown (fourth from left) and Patricia Taylor (fourth from right) shortly after their investiture as Members of the Order of Canada, accompanied by their spouses and fellow staff from the Canadian Embassy in Tehran who had previously been invested into the Order of Canada. Maureen McTeer, wife of Prime Minister Joe Clark, is on the far right.

Above: HRH the Duke of Edinburgh being invested as a Companion of the Order of Canada by Governor General David Johnston.

Right: HRH the Duke of Edinburgh signing the Register of the Order of Canada.

By 2002 appointments to the honorary division of the Order had become more frequent. American Frank Gehry, the noted architect who had been born in Toronto, became the first non-royal or non-head of state to be made an honorary Companion. British designer Tanya Moiseiwitsch, whose artistic contributions to the Stratford Festival extended back more than fifty years, was made an honorary Officer. Former Czech president Václav Havel and former secretary general of the UN Boutros Boutros-Ghali were made honorary Companions in 2003, and the Aga Khan IV was appointed in 2005. In addition to the six honorary Companions, nine honorary Officers and five honorary Members have been appointed.

In 2013 a third division was added to the Order, that of extraordinary membership. The addition of the extraordinary division to the Order was made to allow for the appointment of members of the Canadian Royal Family to the Order, and also to correct a longstanding anomaly whereby the governor general and the vice-regal spouse were appointed to the general division of the Order without deducting their appointments from the numerical limit on membership. In 2013 all living governors general and vice-regal spouses were transferred to the extraordinary division of the Order.

The first member of the Royal Family to be admitted to the Order in the extraordinary division was His Royal Highness the Duke of Edinburgh in 2013. The Duke had first been nominated for the Order in 1967; however, there was no mechanism to appoint members of the Royal Family, so while his nomination file grew in size he could not be admitted to the Order. On several occasions the offer was made to appoint him as an ex-officio Companion of the Order as the Queen's consort — each time he refused, saying that he wanted to earn the appointment and not simply be given it by virtue of his position.

His Royal Highness the Prince Philip, Duke of Edinburgh, has long embodied dignity, loyalty and service to others. He has known eleven Canadian governors general and eleven prime ministers, and has been present at events which have shaped our nation, including the signing of the Canadian Charter of Rights and Freedoms. His Royal Highness has a keen interest in the personal development of young people and, through the Duke of Edinburgh's Award, has helped to advance the community engagement and personal achievement of young Canadians. In addition, he has long held close ties with Canada's Armed Forces, which have recognized his service with the unique ranks of honorary admiral and general. Through his many visits to Canada, both on his own and with Her Majesty the Queen, he has shown his lasting concern for our country and for Canadians.[91]

As with every Canadian honour, membership in the Order of Canada can be revoked, and this has occurred on a number of occasions. The ignominious terminations have consisted of Alan Eagleson (1998), David Ahenakew (2005), T. Sher Singh (2008), Steve Fonyo (2010), Garth Drabinsky (2012), and Conrad Black (2013). There have also been nine resignations from the Order.

In 1988 another change was made to the Canadian honours system, with the addition of the Canadian Heraldic Authority (CHA) to the Chancellery of Honours. The CHA grants arms, flags, and badges to Canadian citizens and institutions on behalf of the Crown. Prior to its creation, Canadians had to apply to officials in the United Kingdom at the College of Arms in London or the Court of the Lord Lyon in Scotland to obtain a grant of arms. With the patriation of heraldry to Canadian soil, another element of the Crown's symbolic functions was Canadianized. Since 1988 the CHA has been a world leader in incorporating Aboriginal symbols, ensuring that there is no gender differentiation in the type of grants of arms made to men and women, and highlighting Canada's rich symbolic diversity.

EIGHT

SPECIAL EVENTS, INVESTITURES, AND ANNIVERSARIES

For every recipient and their family, receiving word that they have or a loved one has been appointed to the Order is a special event — one of those moments in life that is joyously recounted for years to come. Notice of appointment was originally sent via a formal letter; however, in recent times, soon-to-be-appointed members are called by an official from the Chancellery of Honours or, on occasion, the governor general. Of course, it is the investiture and dinner that follows which mark the culmination of the formal event. In the history of the Order over the past fifty years, a number of special events and anniversaries have been celebrated — both officially by the Government of Canada and, unofficially, by those who played a role in the establishment or operation of the Order. Just as the membership of the Order of Canada is a living society of merit and fraternity of achievement, the Order itself, and those who are responsible for it, have given the institution a life of its own.

As we saw in chapter six, the first investiture took place in the governor general's study at Rideau Hall and was presided over by the Queen, with the Duke of Edinburgh, Prime Minister Pearson, and a number of officials present for the historic occasion. Since that time, with the exception of two governors general, every Chancellor of the Order has been personally invested by the Queen as a Companion of the Order. David Johnston, having been appointed a Companion twelve years before being sworn in to office, was only presented with his insignia as a Commander of the Order of Military Merit and Commander of the Order of Merit of the Police Forces by the Queen at Balmoral Castle in Scotland. The Queen has also invested a few others, notably during her August 1973

RIGHT: Jules Léger being invested as a
Companion of the Order of Canada
by the Queen at Rideau Hall.

BELOW: Jules Léger's group of
miniature medals.

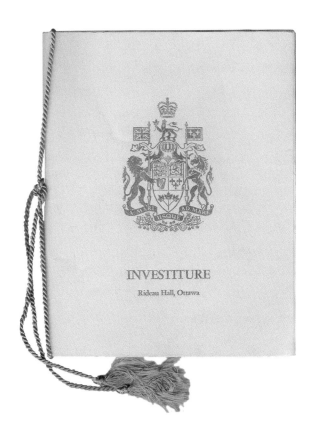

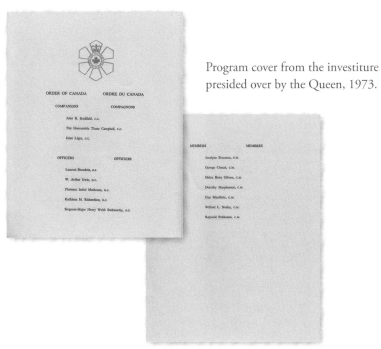

Program cover from the investiture presided over by the Queen, 1973.

tour as part of the Commonwealth Heads of Government Meeting that was being held in Ottawa. In the ballroom at Rideau Hall, the Queen invested three Companions of the Order, including the future governor general Jules Léger, five Officers, and seven Members. Fifteen recipients of the Canadian decorations for bravery and the Order of Military Merit were also invested by the Queen at the same ceremony.

Two other special presentations related to the insignia worn by the Queen as Sovereign of the Order, and the governor general as Chancellor, were made shortly after the Order's establishment. Traditionally, senior officials of an order receive a special insignia to denote their position. The idea for special Order of Canada insignia originated with Major General Colquhoun of Britain's Central Chancery of the Orders of Knighthood. Following the completion of the insignia for the first Companions and recipients of the Medal of Service, graphic designer Bruce Beatty set to work designing special insignia for the Queen and her Canadian representative.

The first of these to be completed was the chancellor's chain that was presented to Roland Michener at Rideau Hall by E.F. Brown, the Acting Master of the Royal Canadian Mint, on December 22, 1968, and worn at Order of Canada investitures ever since. The chancellor's chain of the Order was first incorporated into the governor general's installation ceremony in 1979, when Edward Schreyer was sworn in as Canada's twenty-second governor general and the third Chancellor of the Order of Canada. The chain was crafted by the Royal Canadian Mint's Marvin Cook and Argo Aarand in their spare time and over lunch hours. Made up of twenty-three devices linked together by a double row of

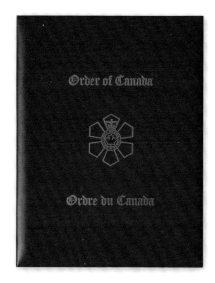

ABOVE: Case for the Chancellor's Chain.

RIGHT: Chancellor's Chain of the Order of Canada.

Governor General David Johnston being presented with the Chancellor's Chains of the Order of Canada, Order of Military Merit, and Order of Merit of the Police Forces at his installation ceremony, 2010.

small gold links, the chain displays twelve devices that are miniature replicas of the white snowflake. Alternating with these are ten devices, each in the form of a red maple leaf on a white background encircled by the red annulus bearing the motto of the Order. The chain is completed by a centre device in the form of the shield from the Royal Arms of Canada surmounted by the Royal Crown.

The concept for the Sovereign's Badge of the Order had been decided upon by August 1967 at a meeting between the officials of the Order.[92] By 1970 Beatty had designed a Sovereign's Badge: an 18-carat-gold snowflake enamelled in white with a large square diamond set between each of the arms, with a maple leaf in the centre surrounded by an annulus, both set with calibre rubies pavé. On the annulus is the motto in pierced gold. Above the snowflake is a gold St. Edward's crown with the cap of maintenance enamelled red and the ermine enamelled white. The arches are set with twenty-one diamonds, with a larger one in the orb. The base is set with a sapphire, two emeralds, and two rubies. The Sovereign's Badge was manufactured by William Summers of Garrard & Company, the Crown Jewellers. Governor

THE SOVEREIGN'S BADGE
OF THE
ORDER OF CANADA

The Sovereign's Badge
of
THE ORDER OF CANADA

AN 18 CARAT GOLD SIX ARM CROSS ENAMELLED WHITE WITH A LARGE SQUARE DIAMOND BETWEEN EACH OF THE ARMS. IN THE CENTRE A MAPLE LEAF SURROUNDED BY AN ANNULUS BOTH SET WITH CALIBRE-RUBIES PAVÉ. ON THE ANNULUS IS THE MOTTO OF PIERCED GOLD. ABOVE THE CROSS A GOLD ST. EDWARD CROWN WITH THE CAP OF MAINTENANCE ENAMELLED RED AND THE ERMINE ENAMELLED WHITE. THE ARCHES ARE SET WITH 21 DIAMONDS WITH A LARGER ONE IN THE ORB. THE BASE IS SET WITH A SAPPHIRE, TWO EMERALD AND TWO RUBIES.

PRESENTED TO HER MAJESTY BY GOVERNOR GENERAL ROLAND MICHENER
AT BUCKINGHAM PALACE ON JUNE 23RD 1970.

THIS PAGE: Designs for the Sovereign's Badge of the Order of Canada.

JOYCE M. BRYANT, CM, BEM (1922–)

The first employee of the Order of Canada secretariat, Joyce Bryant had served in the Royal Canadian Air Force during the Second World War. Returning to Canada in 1946, she took a job with the office of the secretary to the governor general. A native of Winnipeg, Manitoba, aside from a seven-year period working for Vincent Massey following his retirement as governor general, Bryant would spend her entire post-war career at Rideau Hall. Her efficiency and exemplary service during the war was recognized with the British Empire Medal, and in 1973 she was made a Member of the Order of Canada. A close friend of Bruce Beatty and Esmond Butler, she would hold a number of Order of Canada anniversary events at her home in Ottawa.

General and Mrs. Michener were visiting Britain to attend the tercentenary of the Hudson's Bay Company when, on June 23, 1970, after lunch with the Queen at Buckingham Palace, Michener presented his host with the Sovereign's Badge of the Order of Canada. The Queen is said to have been most impressed with the design and delighted to receive the insignia. A new insignia will have to be produced for a male sovereign, as the sovereign's insignia created for Her Majesty is only intended for wear on a bow, and is a reduced size to allow for it to be worn without difficulty on a dress.

Tenth Anniversary Medallion,
obverse and reverse.

QUEEN ELIZABETH II, QUEEN OF CANADA (1926–)

Founding Sovereign of the Order of Canada, the Queen took a deep interest in the establishment of the Order. As Canada's head of state and the fount of all national honours, the Queen has played a role in the creation of all Canadian orders, decorations, and medals since 1967. It was the Queen who approved the insignia designs and invested the first member of the Order, Governor General Roland Michener. Shortly after ascending to the throne, the Queen personally appointed the renowned neurosurgeon Dr. Wilder Penfield to the Order of Merit. She had some frustration in not being able to recognize other Canadians with senior honours, such as the refusal of Prime Ministers St. Laurent and Diefenbaker to allow Vincent Massey to be appointed as a Knight of the Order of the Garter in the late 1950s. Early in the history of the Order, the Queen's private secretary noted that the regular submission of Order of Canada lists provided an "admirable way for the Queen to keep in touch with the activities of Canadians who have in various ways played an outstanding part in the life of the country."

- 2 -

On April seventeenth at last
    The P.M. gave his speech -
Then Blackburn, Smyth et al worked fast;
    The wheels began to turn.

Alas, some steno slipped one day
    In typing out the Motto -
The Hebrew's verse had gone astray,
    And "fornication" hovered.

But chaste and virgin now once more,
    We made July the sixth,
When great Canadians (plus fourscore)
    Composed the premier list.

We settled first for grades but two,
    With "Courage" on the side,
But found too many "Who's" were "Who" -
    So added level three.

- 3 -

Now Comps. and Offs. and Members all
    Are "pinned" within the fold,
And service great and service small
    Is honoured with a Badge.

Investitures a score we've seen
    Since that first one was held,
And every discipline has been
    Included in the group.

A lot of laughs, a tear or two
    Has flavoured each event.
But overall, I think it's true -
    We've really had a ball.

B.W.B.   J.T.

Tenth Anniversary Poem, written by Bruce Beatty and Joyce Bryant.

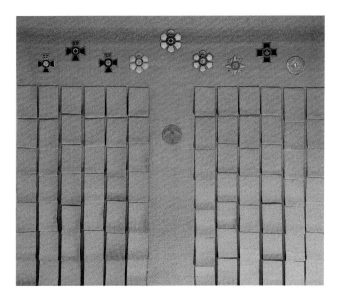

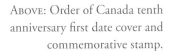

ABOVE: Order of Canada tenth anniversary first date cover and commemorative stamp.

TOP LEFT: Order of Canada commemorative dinner plate used at the Order of Canada dinners from 1978 on.

TOP RIGHT: Order of Canada and Canadian Honours tapestry commissioned for the Order's tenth anniversary.

A number of special events were held in connection with the tenth anniversary of the Order, which also coincided with the Queen's Silver Jubilee in 1977. In honour of the decennial anniversary of the Order, Canada Post issued a commemorative stamp, and the governor general commissioned the Royal Canadian Mint to strike a special gold medallion, which was then given to each of the one thousand living Canadian members who had been invested into the Order since 1967.

Joyce Bryant held a potluck cocktail party in honour of the Order's tenth anniversary at her home on Creighton Street in Ottawa.

This was attended by many of those who had been involved with the Order's first years of operation. It was a black tie and decorations affair at which each guest was first presented with a large cardboard cutout of the Order, which was worn on the left lapel. Along with a decorated cake, a comical poetry reading was performed at which a poem detailing the history of the Order's development was read. It was a jovial affair that would be remembered for many years to come, one that thankfully included the longtime investiture photographer John Evans and his wife Dody, who chronicled the event for posterity.

The Order's tenth anniversary also saw the commissioning of a commemorative dinner plate by renowned English china producer Spode. Although not delivered until 1978, the gold-rimmed white porcelain plate displays the Companion's insignia in the central field and is surrounded by a flowing border of natural maple leaves in gold and a red outer border. Since they were delivered, these plates have been used to serve dessert at the investiture dinner. A commemorative tapestry by noted artist Micheline Beauchemin, OC, OQ, depicting the insignia of the Order, along with the insignia of the Order of Military Merit and Canadian decorations for bravery, was also commissioned to celebrate the Order's decennial anniversary.

A group shot of Rideau Hall staff involved with the Order of Canada, taken in 1979, on the occasion of the twenty-fifth Order of Canada investiture.

Renowned composer and conductor Sir Ernest MacMillan was one of the first to be invested in a place other than Rideau Hall. MacMillan was not in the most robust health when he was appointed to the Order in 1969, and being quite comfortable in his Toronto home, he requested that the investiture be held there so he would not have to travel to Ottawa. Roland Michener invested Sir Ernest with his insignia in the living room of his home on November 19, 1969, and a small celebratory party was held following the formalities. Accounts from those in attendance and photos of the investiture recount that Sir Ernest was in reasonable health at the time and was quite excited with the idea of having a private affair to which he could invite family and friends — much more than the two guests that investees were permitted to bring to normal investitures. Another Canadian knight, who also happened to be a First World War air ace and super-spy of the Second World War, Sir William Stephenson, "The Man Called Intrepid," would be invested at his home in Bermuda by Governor General Edward Schreyer in February 1980. Investitures are also occasionally held at other government houses across Canada or at a recipient's bedside on account of illness or infirmity. Frank Sobey was invested as an Officer of the Order of Canada in the ballroom at Government House in Halifax by then-Lieutenant Governor Alan R. Abraham in October 1985, a short two weeks before his death.

The most poignant special investiture was held at the city hall in Port Coquitlam, British Columbia, on September 19, 1980, where Terry Fox was invested as a Companion of the Order — the youngest person ever to be appointed to its highest level. Recognized for his Marathon of Hope to benefit the Canadian Cancer Society, which saw him embark

No. 38, Vol. 114

The Canada Gazette
Part I

OTTAWA, SATURDAY, SEPTEMBER 20, 1980

N° 38, Vol. 114

La Gazette du Canada
Partie I

OTTAWA, SAMEDI 20 SEPTEMBRE 1980

GOVERNMENT HOUSE

OTTAWA

ORDER OF CANADA

The Governor General, the Right Honourable EDWARD SCHREYER, in his capacity as Chancellor and Principal Companion of the Order of Canada, has appointed the following Canadian, who has been recommended for such appointment by the Advisory Council of the Order,

To be a Companion of the Order of Canada

Terrance Stanley FOX

Witness the Seal of the Order of Canada this fourteenth day of September, one thousand nine hundred and eighty

ESMOND BUTLER
Secretary General
Order of Canada

RÉSIDENCE DU GOUVERNEUR GÉNÉRAL

OTTAWA

ORDRE DU CANADA

Le Gouverneur général, le très honorable EDWARD SCHREYER, en sa qualité de Chancelier et de Compagnon principal de l'Ordre du Canada, a nommé le Canadien dont le nom suit, selon la recommandation du Conseil consultatif de l'Ordre,

Compagnon de l'Ordre du Canada

Terrance Stanley FOX

Témoin le Sceau de l'Ordre du Canada ce quatorzième jour de septembre mil neuf cent quatre-vingt

Le secrétaire général
de l'Ordre du Canada
ESMOND BUTLER

ABOVE: *Canada Gazette* entry announcing the appointment of Terry Fox to the Order of Canada.

TOP RIGHT: Terry Fox, the youngest person ever appointed as a Companion of the Order of Canada, 1980.

on a cross-Canada run, Fox did much to raise funds to aid cancer research and also to reduce the stigma that had long been associated with the disease. The result has been contributions to cancer research amounting to more than thirteen million dollars at the time of his investiture. Terry's example has, in turn, given new courage to those across the land who struggle against disease and infirmity. By his disregard for his own pain and by his devotion to a greater cause, Terry embodies the motto of the Order of Canada — "They desire a better country."[93] Following the investiture, the affable, yet somewhat overwhelmed Fox commented, "If I've had a part in pulling the whole country together, each province, I really, that really makes me feel good."[94] Nine months later Fox would succumb to the disease he did so much in life to overcome. Having spawned one of the greatest philanthropic movements in Canadian history, he remains an outstanding example of the Order's ethos.

In 1992 a number of significant commemorations took place in conjunction with the 125th anniversary of Confederation, the 40th anniversary of the Queen's accession to the throne, and the 25th anniversary of the Order's establishment. As part of Canada 125, a pair of stained-glass windows was unveiled at Government House in Ottawa to commemorate these important anniversaries, and also the 40th anniversary of the appointment of the first Canadian as governor general. The royal window depicts

LEFT: The Royal Window unveiled at Rideau Hall as part of the 125th anniversary of Confederation. The Royal Arms include the motto circlet of the Order of Canada for the first time.

RIGHT: The Vice-Regal Window, unveiled at the same time as the Royal Window, commemorates the fortieth anniversary of Canadians being appointed as governors general.

the Royal Arms of Canada with the shield surrounded by the motto of the Order of Canada, as well as the insignia of Sovereign of the Order of Canada — two elements which also highlighted the 25th anniversary of the Order. The accompanying vice-regal window also includes a representation of the insignia of Companion of the Order, alluding to the fact that the governor general is the Chancellor and Principal Companion of the Order. The commemorative medal issued for Canada 125, designed by Bruce Beatty, also depicted the shield from the Canadian coat of arms surrounded by the circlet and motto of the Order.[95] All living members of the Order were awarded this commemorative medal.

A special pair of commemorative stamps was also issued by Canada Post: the first commemorating the Order and the second memorializing the life of Roland Michener, former governor general and first Chancellor of the Order.

Two years later, the Royal Arms of Canada were augmented to formally include the motto circlet of the Order of Canada, with the drawing being undertaken by Cathy Bursey-Sabourin, Fraser Herald of the Canadian Heraldic Authority. The addition of the motto circlet was approved by the Queen on July 12, 1994.

LEFT: The 125th anniversary of Confederation Medal, obverse.

RIGHT: The reverse of the 125th anniversary of Confederation Medal, displaying the motto circlet of the Order of Canada.

Along with the 25th anniversary of the Order of Canada, 1992 also marked the 125th anniversary of Confederation. As part of the celebrations held at Rideau Hall, Governor General Ray Hnatyshyn brought together many of the former household staff to share their memories of life in the vice-regal household. The silver jubilee of the Order included a special investiture held in the ballroom at Rideau Hall on October 21, 1992, just a month shy of the anniversary of when the original Companions and recipients of the Medal of Service stood in the very same spot to receive their insignia. Throughout his time as governor general, Order of Canada events were amongst Governor General Hnatyshyn's favourite functions. In his address at the end of the investiture, Hnatyshyn noted:

> Members of the Order of Canada have reminded all Canadians that our country's greatest wealth does not lie in its resources, its trees or water, its wildlife — however splendid these are. It rests in our people, in the spirit captured by the motto of the Order of Canada — "They desire a better country." Each of you not only desires a better country, you have acted to *make* a better country.

Daniel Roland Michener
1900-1991

Order of Canada / Ordre du Canada
1967-1992

Stamps commemorating the Order of Canada's twenty-fifth anniversary in 1992 and the life of Governor General Roland Michener.

Royal Arms of Canada, 1994, including the Order of Canada motto circlet.

ABOVE: Then–Governor General
Michaëlle Jean (left) and Jean-Daniel
Lafond (centre) celebrate the Order's
fortieth anniversary, 2007.

RIGHT: The Order of Canada's
fortieth anniversary cake.

Far from resting on their laurels, many recipients have been inspired to become even more energetically involved in dealing with major social, cultural, and educational causes. It is a reminder, if one is still needed, of the diversity of this country and the ingenuity and energy of its people.[96]

At the fortieth anniversary investiture, two of the first people appointed to the Order, artist Alex Colville and Dr. Jacques Genest, were in attendance, along with the designer of the insignia of the Order, Bruce Beatty. They spoke about some of the first Rideau Hall employees to work on the Order, Joyce Bryant and Tony Smyth, and other members of the household staff who were present for the first investiture in November 1967. Governor General Michaëlle Jean reflected, "We are very modest, very reserved in our self-appreciation. I have seen it time and again in my travels across the country…. Those of you being honoured today are those role models. Never underestimate the hope that you inspire in our society. Through your actions and your ideas, you encourage us to push ourselves and to discover how much power we have to change the world."[97] It was at this special investiture ceremony that the master chef at Rideau Hall unveiled a unique cake, shaped and decorated like the insignia of the Order.

The Order's fiftieth anniversary will be marked by a commemorative coin from the Royal Canadian Mint, a stamp from Canada Post, and a number of commemorative events, along with a special fiftieth anniversary investiture ceremony. A series of cross-Canada events will also be held by the Walrus Foundation, with members of the Order of Canada attending each.

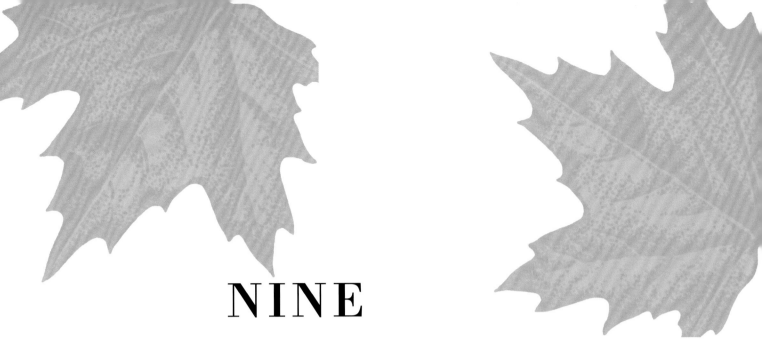

NINE

THE JULY 1922 CREW:
BUTLER, BEATTY, AND BRYANT

The establishment of the Order of Canada involved a small cadre of key players who developed the details of the new national institution; this included the Order's letters patent, constitution, ribbon, insignia, certificate, pamphlets, procedures, and investiture ceremony. The involvement of cabinet ministers and senior officials was peripheral and the minutiae of the Order's actual creation and operation was left to a few officials of modest station. Aside from the Queen, Governor General Roland Michener, former Governor General Vincent Massey, and Prime Minister Pearson, the proverbial cast of characters numbered a baker's dozen. Pearson had his "honours team," which was made up of Esmond Butler, Jack Hodgson, John Matheson, and Michael Pitfield. Monitoring all the progress was Gordon Robertson, the Clerk of the Privy Council.

Butler would go on to be the Order's first secretary general, while Pitfield, then a senior adviser in the Privy Council Office, would later become Clerk of the Privy Council and eventually be summoned to the Senate. Edythe I. MacDonald was one of the Department of Justice's first female counsels and a future provincial court judge. Jack Hodgson was an adviser in the Prime Minister's Office. John Halstead was a young diplomat who would go on to serve as Canada's ambassador to NATO, and was also from the Department of External Affairs. The rest of the team included Anthony Smyth and Robert Blackburn — Smyth, who would go on to serve as deputy secretary to the governor general, and Blackburn, who would serve as assistant deputy minister in a number of federal departments before becoming a vice-president with SNC Lavelin; Member of Parliament John Matheson, who had previously played a part in the adoption of the Maple Leaf flag; retired

The July 1922 Crew — Bruce Beatty, Esmond Butler, and Joyce Bryant — in Bryant's kitchen during a tenth anniversary party for the Order of Canada.

Esmond Butler blows out the candles on a tenth anniversary Order of Canada cake, 1977.

Royal Canadian Navy pilot Roger de C. Nantel, who became the first Registrar of the Order and later director of honours; Conrad Swan, a Canadian working at the College of Arms in London, who in later life was knighted and made head of England's heraldic authority; Flight Sergeant Bruce Beatty of the Department of National Defence's ceremonial branch, who would go on to design many Canadian orders, decorations, and medals; and Joyce Bryant (née Turpin), the first employee of the Order of Canada, who worked for every governor general from Lord Alexander to Ray Hnatyshyn.

Of all these people, three in particular had an enduring involvement in the Order of Canada, its administration and evolution. Bruce Beatty, Joyce Bryant, and Esmond Butler had the longest association with the Order. All born within weeks of each other in 1922, they were dubbed the "July 1922 Crew." Later in life Joyce Bryant would joke that they were the "B Team," given their shared birthdays, the fact their surnames all started with the letter B, and the close friendship that developed between the trio throughout their lifetimes. All three saw service in the Second World War and collectively devoted 110 years of service to the governor general's office — much of that time focused on matters related to honours and the Order of Canada.

The first of the three to arrive at Rideau Hall was Muriel Joyce Bryant. The daughter of a CN Rail clerk, Bryant was born in Winnipeg, Manitoba. She spent her youth there, until the untimely death of her father in 1937, when her mother returned to England where they would remain until after the Second World War. Bryant's mother worked as a censor for MI5, while Bryant joined the Women's Division of the Royal Canadian Air Force. It was there that her organizational and secretarial skills, not

Bruce Beatty (left) and Joyce Bryant (right) with then–Governor General Roméo LeBlanc (centre) at an event in honour of the Order's thirtieth anniversary.

to mention her ability to interact with all manner of senior officials, were acquired, earning her a rare British Empire Medal (Military Division) in the process.

Following a distinguished career in the RCAF, which saw her working in the medical division of the RCAF at Canadian Military Headquarters in London, Bryant was demobilized in 1946. Shortly thereafter she was hired onto the household staff of Government House in Ottawa to serve as a stenographer to then–Governor General Field Marshal Lord Alexander of Tunis. Aside from a stint as secretary to Vincent Massey following his retirement as governor general, Bryant would remain at Rideau Hall for nearly forty years in various positions, most notably as the first employee of the Order of Canada secretariat, which would later be called the Chancellery of Honours.

Following Vincent Massey's departure from office in 1959, Bryant followed him to his country estate at Batterwood, near Port Hope, Ontario, where she assisted the former governor general with preparing his memoirs, dealing with correspondence, and facing the challenges of continuing on in public life after departing vice-regal service. As plans for the Order of Canada came together, Esmond Butler was faced with the task of finding a suitable candidate to administer the clerical day-to-day operations of the new institution.

Unlike today, all nomination forms and summaries for the Advisory Council were prepared manually — without the aid of a computer. A manual index card system was developed to handle the biographical details of all those nominated for and appointed to the Order.

Conveniently for Butler, shortly after Canada Day and the extensive Centennial celebrations that were held in Ottawa, Bryant went to meet with him about the possibility of returning to work at Rideau Hall. Aware that Mr. Massey's schedule and clerical requirements were ebbing with the completion of his memoirs, Butler was delighted with the prospect of having Bryant return to Ottawa to work in the household — in particular to assist with the setup of the Order of Canada.

Bryant was already well aware of the Order's establishment, having been present for some of the early discussions that took place between Butler, Michael Pitfield, and Massey earlier in the summer of 1966. In August 1967, Bryant departed Port Hope to return to Ottawa and Rideau Hall, where she would become the first full-time employee devoted to the Order of Canada.

Bryant would be appointed a Member of the Order of Canada in 1973 "for her dedication through her service at Government House during the tenure of five Governors General."[98] Amusingly, the Advisory Council and staff at Rideau Hall had to go to great lengths to prevent Bryant from learning of her own nomination — she was, after all, responsible for processing all nominations and the paperwork that was reviewed by the Advisory Council. This took a great deal of effort, and on the fateful day when she was informed of her appointment as a Member of the Order, Roland Michener called her. "I need you in my office — right away!"[99] Off she dashed to the governor general's oak-panelled study, where she truly believed that she was going to be given her pink slip.

After all, it was the first time His Excellency or any of his predecessors had ever addressed her with such sternness. Upon entering the room, she was startled to see both her supervisor, Registrar of the Order Roger de C. Nantel, and the secretary to the governor general, Esmond Butler, glaring at her in an unpleasant manner. Bryant noticed a letter in the governor general's hand and her mind raced: *Of course they aren't going to fire me — that would be much too messy. They'd drafted a letter of resignation for me to*

Joyce Bryant's group of medals, including the Order of Canada.

July 14, 1982.

Dear Joyce,

This is just a note to thank you for your letter dated June 25th with which you enclosed a copy of your report on the contract you had undertaken for the Chancellery of Canadian Orders and Decorations. You will remember that we discussed all this when you came to see me recently, but it is only in the last few days that I have had a chance to have a look at the report.

When we asked you to undertake this project, we were very uncertain about our records and your research seems to confirm that a great deal of sorting and reclassification was necessary. I now get the impression that our files are in very good order and I am most grateful for the very meticulous job you have done. I am sure that researchers and those requiring information in the future will bless you. There was no one else who had the necessary knowledge as you were associated with the Canadian System of Honours from the beginning and I am so grateful that you were prepared to take on this enterprise.

There are still some things to be done to ensure that our House is in good order and I shall speak to Mr. Nantel soon about your recommendations.

With kindest regards and renewed thanks,

Yours sincerely,

Esmond Butler,
Secretary to the Governor General

Mrs. Joyce Bryant,
102 Crichton Street,
Ottawa, Ontario.
K1M 1V9

sign.... Despair flooded her soul.[100] As the blood drained from her face, the governor general began reading the letter: "I am pleased to inform you that the Advisory Council of the Order of Canada has recommended to the Governor General that you be appointed a Member of the Order of Canada." Slightly agog and in a state of shock, Bryant burst into tears and then fell over the arm of a chair and landed on the floor with legs in the air. It was almost certainly the most unconventional Order of Canada appointment announcement ever made.

Throughout her time working for the Order of Canada, Bryant regularly brought those involved with the administration of the Order together on various occasions, such as the twenty-fifth investiture and the tenth anniversary of the Order. For the Order's tenth anniversary, she held a cocktail party at her home in Ottawa for all those associated with the honour, and she wrote a decennial anniversary poem about the Order and its history. When Esmond Butler was invested into the Order in 1989, she hosted a party in his honour. To this day she remains a special repository of anecdotes and stories about the early days of the Canadian honours system and the Order of Canada in particular. Retiring from Rideau Hall in 1981, she would shortly thereafter be called back to work for the Chancellery of Honours and on a number of special projects — finally retiring from vice-regal service in 1992.

The next member of the July 1922 Crew to join the household staff at Rideau Hall was Esmond Unwin Butler, a man who would do more to define the office of the governor general in Canada than any of his predecessors or successors. Butler modernized and

ABOVE: Letter from Butler to Bryant about the Order of Canada's archives.

LEFT: Esmond Butler's official portrait as Secretary to the Governor General.

helped to bring a Victorian institution into the twentieth century. Also from Manitoba, Butler was born in Wawanesa to an Anglican priest who had immigrated to Canada from England shortly before the start of the First World War. After attending high school in Weston, Ontario, Butler joined the Royal Canadian Naval Volunteer Reserve in the summer of 1942 and would see service on the Atlantic and in less exotic postings such as Regina, Saskatchewan. Rising to the rank of lieutenant commander, and it being noted that he was an "intelligent leader … his officer like qualities are high," senior officers were keen to retain him in the RCN; however, Butler had other aspirations. Following demobilization, Butler undertook a history degree at the University of Toronto and went on to take a degree at the Institute of International Studies at the University of Geneva in Switzerland. Having greatly enhanced his French language skills in Switzerland, Butler worked as a reporter for United Press International (UPI) in Geneva, becoming its resident expert on Canada, writing articles on Canadian trade and commerce.

In 1953 he returned to Canada and the Department of Trade and Commerce, where he served as an information officer. In 1955 he was lured away from the civil service by Lionel Massey, who was secretary to the governor general at the time. Butler was hired as assistant secretary to the governor general, with a specific focus on dealing with the press. As the first Canadian-born governor general since the French Regime, Vincent Massey was under intense scrutiny, and in certain quarters the press was keen to pounce on his patrician manner and rigid adherence to protocol. In essence, Butler became the first press secretary to a governor general.

Following the end of the Queen's highly successful 1957 Royal Tour of Canada, which saw Canada's Parliament opened by a reigning monarch for the first time, Butler was approached by the Queen's private secretary, Sir Michael Adeane, to take up the post of assistant press secretary to the Queen at Buckingham Palace. A decade later, Adeane would himself play an important part in securing the Queen's approval for the establishment of the Order of Canada.

It was during the Queen's 1959 Royal Tour of Canada that Butler was approached to return to Canada to head up the office of the secretary to the governor general. The newly appointed governor general, General Georges Vanier, was in need of a new secretary and wanted someone he could trust implicitly. Another candidate had been advanced by Prime Minister Diefenbaker, but he was viewed as being too connected to the Prime Minister's Office, thus Vanier was anxious to have his own choice as chief adviser at Rideau Hall. While this did not go over well with the prime minister, Butler came on the recommendation of none other than Her Majesty the Queen — leaving Diefenbaker no option but to accept Vanier's choice.

Butler took up the role of secretary to the governor general, a position that traces its roots to 1603 and the first private secretary to a governor in Acadia. He immediately commenced a program of modernizing not only communications and the relationship with the press, but all manner of administrative and organizational details that helped to greatly increase the efficiency and effectiveness of the vice-regal household. As the

Party celebrating Esmond Butler's investiture as an Officer of the Order of Canada, c. 1989.

first secretary general of the Order of Canada, he was in a unique position to establish and oversee the development of not only the Order, but the broader Canadian honours system that we know today. Butler oversaw the transformation of the role of the governor general, from one often perceived to be a British official ensconced in official Ottawa, into an accessible public figure who was actively engaged in the affairs of the nation — well beyond the perfunctory constitutional duties and ceremonials that surround Rideau Hall and its occupants.

In a period when Canada was adopting an increasing number of new symbols and traditions, Butler was central in all matters touching upon the monarchy, its function, and its symbols throughout Canada. From the establishment of the Order of Canada and the broader Canadian honours system, through to the delegation of many of the Queen's responsibilities to the governor general, Butler deftly advised a succession of governors general, prime ministers, and Clerks of the Privy Council through the nuances of changing the conventions and critical aspects of the machinery of government. Throughout the constitutional discussions of the 1970s and 1980s, Butler was a constant adviser on all matters related to the roles of the Queen, governor general, and lieutenant governors. He was also instrumental in tempering changes made to the role of the Queen and governor general during the 1970s, often working behind closed doors as a firm defender of the Crown's position as a Canadian institution — not simply one borrowed from Britain.

As the longest-serving secretary in the Commonwealth, Butler was a resource not only for his Canadian colleagues, but to his peers in Australia, New Zealand, and the United Kingdom. He played a role in the establishment of the Australian honours system in

1975, and the modernization of many of the lieutenant governors' offices across Canada throughout the 1970s and 1980s. For a generation Butler was the institutional memory of Ottawa for all matters touching upon protocol and the Crown. He would continue in the position for twenty-six years, until 1985, when he was appointed as Canada's Ambassador to Morocco. As comfortable in white tie and tails as in hunting plaid and a wool cap, Butler was a keen angler and naturalist who loved the outdoors.

For his service to the Crown, Butler was made a Commander of the Royal Victorian Order in 1972, the first Canadian to be appointed to the Order following the establishment of the Canadian honours system and the first Canadian to earn the distinction in more than a quarter century. A year after retiring as secretary to the governor general, he was appointed an Officer of the Order of Canada in recognition of his twenty-six years of service "with great distinction as Secretary to five successive Governors General and [as] one of the key developers of the Canadian Honours System."[101] In honour of

Notecard signed by all those who attended Esmond Butler's Order of Canada investiture party.

LEFT: Large cardboard Order of Canada insignia with modified motto presented to Esmond Butler by friends and colleagues.

BELOW: Bruce Beatty holding the newly manufactured Sovereign's insignia of the Order of Military Merit, c. 1973.

Butler's Order of Canada investiture, friends and members of the Rideau Hall staff held a special cocktail party in his honour at Joyce Bryant's house. A special large cardboard Order of Canada insignia was hung around Butler's neck and there was much frivolity and recounting of his service to the Queen and a succession of governors general.

Sadly he would die of ALS in December 1989 at the age of sixty-seven, having just commenced a well-earned retirement that he had hoped to spend in the outdoors. No one person since has served as long on the Advisory Council as Butler, nor has a single individual had as ubiquitous an influence over the Order's development.

The latecomer to the July 1922 Crew was Flight Sergeant Bruce Wilbur Beatty. A native of Tisdale, Saskatchewan, he joined the Royal Canadian Air Force in 1941 and spent his wartime service in Canada, finishing as an air observer. Long interested in badges, buttons, and medals, Beatty began collecting medals in the postwar era, when there was little interest, yet an abundance of material. In 1952 he was assigned to the RCAF's central art section, where he remained until 1959, when he was sent to Metz, France, with the RCAF and NATO. He remained in France for seven years looking after the art requirements for the RCAF and various air attachés posted throughout Europe. Beatty's duties consisted of drawing exercise diagrams for physical fitness manuals, the air force magazine, recruiting posters, and all manner of images required in the age before computer-generated drawings. He would later reflect it was a bit like being a graphic designer for an ad agency. Throughout this time he continued to increase his interest in all manner of insignia, heraldry, and drawing various badges and medals. After returning from Europe in 1966, he joined the Department of National Defence as part of the directorate of ceremonial, which was responsible not only for the design of badges, uniforms, and various accoutrements, but also for military parades and ceremonies.

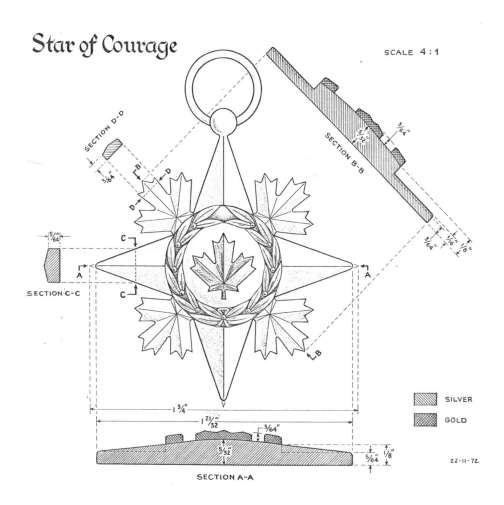

Some of the technical drawings done by Beatty for other elements of the Canadian honours system.

While Beatty's passion was serving as an artist, his regular work also routinely involved assisting with the organization and delivery of military ceremonies — this became a significant part of his job as the Centennial celebrations of 1967 approached. It was a busy time for the directorate as various concepts and ideas were floated for unifying the Royal Canadian Navy, Canadian Army, and Royal Canadian Air Force into a single force. Never one to mince words, the unification of the three services was not one of Beatty's favourite projects; indeed, his willingness to provide unvarnished opinions about such changes became a hallmark of his character throughout his career.

Much to the dismay of his commanding officer, Lieutenant-Colonel N.A. Buckingham, the outspoken and idea-laden Beatty was summoned to the office of none other than Prime Minister Lester B. Pearson. In August 1966 Buckingham appeared in the door of Beatty's office and announced, "The prime minister wants to see you." Beatty's reaction was one of disbelief, and he responded with a wry "Oh sure." Within an hour, Beatty was standing in front of the prime minister, with no idea why. Pearson soon explained: "We are going to institute a Canadian order and you are going to design it."[102]

The prime minister then went on to swear Beatty to secrecy: he was not even permitted to tell his commanding officer what he was working on. This placed Beatty in a very awkward position with his superior. To work on the project, Beatty took extra days of sick leave. Designing the Order of Canada insignia was no easy task. In the end he devised three separate designs, each containing the symbols of the Royal Crown, a maple leaf, and a snowflake. While Pearson chose the ultimate design, it was Beatty's genius that brought forward the elegant and unmistakable snowflake insignia that is so widely recognized today.

In 1970 Beatty retired from the Canadian Armed Forces and became a reservist, and later a cadet instructor. When the Honours Secretariat — what would become the Chancellery of Canadian Honours — was founded in 1972, Beatty was asked to join the staff to take on the design of not only the new honours that would be established, but also Royal Tour badges and various heraldic badges. They also drew upon his expertise with all manner of medals, and their display, mounting, and wearing. It was there he also came into contact with the various manufacturers of badges and medals at the Royal Canadian Mint and other firms in and around Ottawa. This afforded him a unique window into not only the design, but the production of intricate, multi-piece enamelled insignia that were much more akin to jewellery than a military cap badge. He would play a key part in patriating the manufacture of the insignia of the Order of Canada in 1985 when a firm in Quebec became the first Canadian company to produce it.

From 1967 to 2002, Beatty would design almost every order, decoration, and medal in the modern Canadian honours system: from the Order of Canada and Order of Military Merit through to the Military Valour, Bravery, and Meritorious Service Decorations, Exemplary Service Medals, Special Service Medal, Canadian Peacekeeping Service Medal, and many others. He also held the distinction of having attended one hundred Order of Canada investitures over the course of his career. Beatty was appointed a Member of the

Order of Canada in 1990 in recognition of his contribution as "an accomplished graphic artist … he is the creative force behind all of the symbolic representations which make up our Canadian honours system."[103]

Beatty died in March 2011 at the age of eighty-eight. Always impeccably turned out, and a near-constant figure at Order of Canada investitures, his presence was immediately missed. He famously carried in his breast pocket a small index card bearing a detailed list of every investiture he had ever attended — it was a point of pride that he had been involved in not only designing the Order, but also that he had been witness to thousands of Canadians being invested with the snowflake insignia that he so delighted in seeing worn in all its various forms.

TEN

INSIGNIA AND SYMBOLS
OF THE ORDER

The now-familiar white snowflake bedecked with the Royal Crown and a maple leaf has become widely recognized as the insignia of the Order of Canada. The shape and description of orders, decorations, and medals from around the world each tell a specific story, as does the distinctive ribbon, symbols, and mottoes included on a particular insignia. The story behind the insignia of the Order of Canada is one of happenstance, the occasional biblical error, and the arrival at a timeless design that has become a respected national symbol.

The legal mechanics of establishing the Order of Canada, seeking the Queen's approval, getting Cabinet to agree on a structure and method of appointment, and envisioning the Advisory Council, were all parts of the machinery of government that in one form or another takes place with some frequency. The creation of a new national symbol, and determining details such as what the symbol would encompass and display, was not something that many in official Ottawa in 1966–67 were comfortable dealing with. Certainly there were lots of ideas, some of them quite unconventional and symbolically cluttered, but it takes a special sort of talent to design the badge of an order. In addition to questions of just what the Order of Canada would look like and who was to make the insignia, there were other pressing issues, such as precisely what the name of the new honour would be, whether there would be a motto, and other related matters.

Nakaya's photo of the shape that would become the Order of Canada.

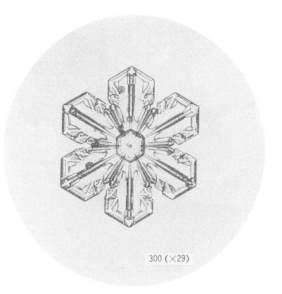

300 (×29)

A set of modern Order of Canada insignia manufactured by the Royal Canadian Mint.

Alan Beddoe's draft design for the Canadian Decoration of Honour.

There was not a great deal of debate about what name the new Order should carry. Earlier attempts to create a Canadian order, dating back to 1866 and Viscount Monck, proposed that it be named the Order of St. Lawrence. This was also the name favoured by Vincent Massey, who had called for a Canadian order of chivalry to be established as part of his 1951 Royal Commission report. It was a name not without some difficulty. Not all Canadians were Christians, so the name would potentially exclude a portion of the population. Added to this was the fact that few Canadians knew of St. Lawrence, and the name was invariably associated with the St. Lawrence River and eastern Canada.

Proposals advanced through the 1940s carried more plausible designations: the Royal Order of Canada, the Order of the Maple Leaf, and even the Royal Elizabethan Order. Later proposals called for a Canadian Decoration of Honour and Canadian Award of Honour, and their later iterations, the King's Canadian Decoration of Honour and the King's Canadian Award of Honour. These proposals were also rejected.

By late 1966, as the Order truly began to take shape, the most popular choice amongst those involved in the project was the "Order of Canada." This name had been suggested several times over the years — by the under-secretary of state, E.H. Coleman, and secretary to the governor general, Major-General H.F.G. Letson, in 1943; in 1945 by the Department of National Defence; and again in 1948 by then–Governor General Viscount Alexander.

"Order of Canada" was favoured for a number of reasons; mainly, it was short and unpretentious in nature, as well as easy to translate into both official languages. John Matheson preferred this name from the beginning, although he considered lengthening it to the Most Honourable

Alan Beddoe's drawings for the Canadian Decoration of Honour. This proposal was made during the Second World War in an effort to establish a national order that was not called an "Order," to circumvent Prime Minister Mackenzie King's phobia of honours.

Order of Canada.[104] Pearson, however, did not want a complex name for the Order and "Most Honourable" was swiftly dropped. The most comical name suggested was the Order of the Beaver;[105] however, this was most likely only put forward in jest.

It was Michael Pitfield who most succinctly advised colleagues and the prime minister on why "Order of Canada" was the ideal name for the new order, stating that it "avoids any religious, chivalrous or regional connotation."[106]

In the October 1966 drafts of the Order's constitution, the honour is referred to as the Order of Canada. The final decision came on September 16, 1966, at the Dorchester Hotel in London.[107] Pearson was visiting Britain to work out some of the details related to the new Order, and while there he had meetings with a variety of British officials, including fellow Canadian Conrad Swan, who was working for the College of Arms. From that meeting forward, every mention of the new honour referred to it as the Order of Canada. When the proposal was presented to Cabinet, there was no objection to the name.

The name determined, the next element of the Order's newfound existence to be decided was the motto. A clerical error would result in an amusing public relations *faux pas* on the part of the Prime Minister's Office when the Order was eventually announced.

Most national orders have a motto that relates to some historic element of the order's history or the ethos behind those who earn the distinction. England's highest and oldest order, the Order of the Garter, has the most notable motto: *Honi soit qui mal y pense* (Evil be to him who evil thinks). France's Légion d'honneur has simply *Honneur et patrie* (Honour and fatherland). Typically, a motto is meant to suggest what the particular order represents. Early proposals for a Canadian order lacked a motto, aside from the national

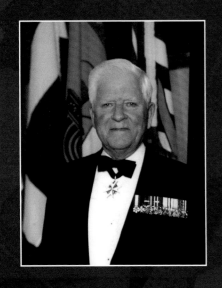

BRUCE W. BEATTY, CM, SOM, CD (1922–2011)

The man responsible for designing the elegant Order of Canada insignia and many of the other orders, decorations, and medals that make up the modern Canadian honours system, Bruce Beatty served in the Royal Canadian Air Force (RCAF) during the Second World War and went on to work for the RCAF's art section following its conclusion. An avid collector of medals and badges, he gained his expertise in design through handling and studying the myriad insignia conferred by countries around the globe. Following his retirement from the Canadian Armed Forces (CAF) in 1970, he became a reservist and worked for the Directorate of Ceremonial, arranging parades and important events for the CAF. In 1972 he joined the staff of what became the Chancellery of Honours, where he remained a fixture until his death in 2011. Over the course of his lifetime, Beatty attended more Order of Canada investitures than anyone else.

motto as displayed on the Royal Arms of Canada — *A mari usque ad mare* (From sea to sea). Other proposals from the 1940s suggested *Acer gerendo* (A productive maple).[108] However, neither of these provided insight into the people and deeds the Order was intended to recognize. Prior to the structure of the Order of Canada being defined, John Matheson had chosen an appropriate motto. There was no opposition to it; among the successive proposals floated in 1966 and 1967, it was the one element that did not change.

During John Matheson's preliminary research into honours at the Library of Parliament, he was confronted with the difficulty of selecting a motto. Philip Laundy, the library's chief of research, pointed out the necessity for a motto; his suggestion was "Our achievement is the nation's achievement."[109] Matheson found the suggestion to be overly bureaucratic, and gave further thought to the matter. A month later he attended a seminar on international affairs in Ottawa. There, Reverend Herbert O'Driscoll of Ottawa's St. John the Evangelist Anglican Church delivered a speech on desiring a better country, using the text of Hebrews 11. O'Driscoll postulated that "We are seeking to make not our country but all countries fulfill their God-given potential, and thereby of course seeking this for our own country."[110] This is most specifically related to Hebrews 11:16: "But now they desire a better country that is heavenly; where for God is not ashamed to be called their God, for he hath established for them a city."

O'Driscoll distilled great meaning from the simple excerpt, relating it to humanity's movement through history: all of us are immigrants; all of us hold the Earth in trust; and all of us are seeking a better country.[111] Matheson immediately latched onto the words, *Desire a better country*. He proposed that the Latin translation, *Desiderantes meliorem patriam,* become the motto of the Order of Canada.[112] This motto gained early acceptance with the prime minister; by October 3, 1966, it had been confirmed and accepted.[113]

One of the more amusing public events in the history of the Order occurred on the day it was announced in Parliament. On April 17, simultaneous with the prime minister's speech, his office issued a press release. Unfortunately, that press release stated that the motto of the Order, *Desiderantes meliorem patriam,* was from Hebrews 12:16. One of the clerical staff had copied the incorrect reference from an early draft of the Order's constitution, which referred to Hebrews 12:16,[114] which states, "Lest there be any fornicator, or profane person, as Esau, who for one morsel of meat sold his birthright." This was rather comical in light of the Munsinger scandal, which was still fresh in the minds of Canadians, and the claims from the opposition parties that Pearson had sold Canada out with the signing of the Auto Pact. Hebrews 12:16 was, in effect, alluding to the political woes of both the Conservatives and Liberals: the one side was accused of fornicating, the other of selling the country out! The opposition leader, John Diefenbaker, never a fan of the Order, commented that, "They can't even quote scripture correctly."[115]

The ribbon of the Order is quite obviously taken from the design and proportions of the national flag of Canada, which is in part modelled on the ribbon of the

ABOVE: Motto of the Order of Canada.

LEFT: Alan Beddoe's draft design for the Canadian Award of Honour.

Canada General Service Medal, 1866–70. The colours red and white were taken from the mantling included in the Royal Arms of Canada, which were granted to the country by King George V in 1921. Earlier proposals for a Canadian honour had highly unusual colour combinations. The 1943 proposal for a Canadian Decoration of Honour and a Canadian Award of Honour called for a ribbon of watered silk in "autumnal brown,"[116] red, yellow, green, purple, and scarlet[117] — a rather garish combination.

Canada General Service Medal, 1866–70, with the now familiar red-and-white ribbon that was eventually used as a template for the Order's ribbon.

The first person to suggest that the combination of red-white-red be used for a Canadian order was Viscount Alexander of Tunis, during his term as governor general. This, along with the inclusion of the Royal Crown and a maple leaf, is one of the few elements taken from earlier proposals of the 1940s and 1950s that managed to succeed in becoming part of the Order of Canada when it was established in 1967. Matheson was not enthusiastic about reusing the flag's proportions as the ribbon of the Order of Canada, and proposed that the ribbon be made "half red and half white,"[118] similar to the bi-colour pattern of the highest non-titular honour in the Commonwealth, the Order of Merit. This was also similar to the ribbon used on the seal of the Royal Proclamation establishing the national flag of Canada in 1965. This emphasized the symbolic link between the national flag and national order. Vincent Massey was nonplussed about this idea and proposed a ribbon along the same lines as Lord Alexander had proposed in 1948. Massey later decided that the ribbon of the Order should be similar in layout to the red-white-red proportions of the new Canadian flag. He even went so far as to have his secretary, Joyce Bryant, sew up a sash of the same proportions to gauge the appearance.[119]

Ribbon taken from the Royal Proclamation announcing the national flag of Canada, c. 1965. This was the red-and-white ribbon Matheson had originally wanted for the Order of Canada.

Pearson showed little interest in such trifles as the colours in the ribbon, provided they were red and white. It was during his July 1966 trip to London that Matheson finally made a decision. While visiting the British medals craftsmen Spink & Son, he met with Mr. E.C. Joslin, a highly regarded expert on decorations. Joslin "suggested a ribbon red, white, red in the flag proportions 1/4, 1/2, 1/4."[120] From that point forward, there was no further debate on the proportions of the ribbon. Since the Order's inception, the ribbon has been produced by Toye, Kenning & Spencer of England — the oldest manufacturers of order and medal ribbon in the world.

An original bolt of Order of Canada ribbon from Toye, Kenning & Spencer. This ribbon dates from 1967.

The design of the actual insignia was undertaken by Flight Sergeant Bruce Beatty, at the time a member of the Department of National Defence's directorate of ceremonial. A graphic artist of considerable talent, Beatty's lifelong contributions to the design of many Canadian orders, decorations, and medals were covered in the previous chapter. Just how Beatty arrived at a white snowflake displaying the Royal Crown and a maple leaf hung from a red-and-white ribbon provides an interesting window into how a variety of Canadian symbols were joined together. The involvement of officials from the prime minister to a young diplomat through to an expert of heraldry and flags and a number of others, not to mention the consideration of a plethora of unattractive designs, makes for an interesting story.

Cadillac hood-ornament style Royal Order of Canada insignia design drawn by Charles Comfort.

The snowflake shape of the Order's insignia finds its distant origins in a Japanese physicist and one of the great students of snow crystals, Ukichiro Nakaya. An expert on crystal formation, Nakaya published an extensive catalogue of thousands of different snowflakes, *Snow Crystals: Natural and Artificial*, which was released in 1954. Never afraid of fieldwork, Nakaya loved the outdoors and snow and all its different properties. Later in life, having spent more than thirty years studying snowflakes, Nakaya would reflect that "snow crystals are letters from heaven."

Having survived the fervour of the flag debate of 1964–65, Lester Pearson had a particular interest in the design of the Order's insignia. In August 1966 Jack Hodgson, one of the prime minister's private secretaries, got in contact with Flight Sergeant Bruce Beatty. Summoned to Pearson's office, Beatty was charged with coming up with three proposals for the Order's insignia. Designing the Order of Canada insignia was no easy task: What shape was the insignia to have? What symbols were to be included? Too many symbols would result in a cluttered, ugly design.

Because there had been previous attempts to create a Canadian Order, there were some existing draft designs, though most of them were quite unsuitable. In 1943 Canadian war artist Dr. Charles Comfort had designed a nine-pointed star symbolizing the nine provinces. In the centre was the shield of the Royal Arms of Canada, surmounted by a crown. Between each of the points was a separate figure "associated with Canadian life":[121] a beaver, pine cone, fish, trillium, bird (dove), maple leaf, sheaf of wheat, shovel and pick, and microscope. At best it was a cluttered and awkward design.

JOHN G.H. HALSTEAD, CM (1922–1998)

Born in Vancouver, British Columbia, John Halstead served with the Royal Canadian Naval Volunteer Reserve during the Second World War in the intelligence section and would join the Department of External Affairs after demobilization in 1946. There, he began a thirty-six-year career that focused primarily on Canada's relationship with Europe. Halstead had the original idea that the Order of Canada insignia should be shaped like a snowflake, not a northern star as had initially been suggested by John Matheson. He went on to serve as Canada's ambassador to NATO and West Germany. Following his retirement from External Affairs, he taught and lectured extensively to students and young Foreign Service officers. In 1996 he was appointed a Member of the Order of Canada.

Some of the unconventional designs undertaken by the Department of National Defence in the 1960s for an Order of Canada and what would eventually become the Order of Military Merit.

Designs for the ill-fated Canadian Award of Honour and the Canadian Decoration of Honour by the noted heraldic artist Alan Beddoe also used a nine-sided insignia. In the centre "three maple leaves conjoined on one stem, proper, superimposed on a laurel wreath seeded proper. And, underneath, the motto *Acer gerendo* in raised letters enamelled in red. The whole ensigned with the Royal Crown in Gold."[122]

The 1960s saw graphic artists at the Department of National Defence put forward a series of designs for neck badges and breast stars for a new Canadian Order. Oddly enough, many of these took their inspiration from a variety of Soviet decorations, and despite emphasizing Canadian symbols such as the maple leaf, the effigy of the Queen, and the national motto, they were totally unsuitable.

Even Vincent Massey had his secretary, Joyce Bryant, take pen to paper to design the new Order of Canada insignia. The Massey version of the Order of Canada was not unattractive; however, it was completely unoriginal. A simple, white-enamelled Maltese cross of eight points "on an oval centre of gold, within which shall appear a scarlet Maple Leaf, inscribed with the word 'CANADA' in gold letters, ensigned with the St. Edward's Crown."[123] Except for the maple leaf in the centre and the "Canada," this insignia was identical to that of the Royal Victorian Order!

ABOVE: The design undertaken by Joyce Bryant at the direction of Vincent Massey, c. 1966.

BELOW: A northern star, the shape originally favoured by Matheson.

Almost everyone involved in the Order of Canada project, regardless of artistic skill, had an opinion of what the insignia should look like. During a reception at the West German embassy, John Matheson met John Halstead. A Foreign Service officer with the Department of External Affairs, Halstead would rise to become Canada's ambassador to NATO and later to West Germany. Somehow, Halstead had learned of Matheson's involvement in founding the Order of Canada. On Monday, November 21, 1966, following a meeting with the West German ambassador,[124] the two men began to discuss possible designs, and Matheson outlined his North Star proposal. Halstead pointed out the possible problems with using a North Star, and then said, "Have you ever thought of a snowflake?"[125] Initially this suggestion struck Matheson as inappropriate: snowflakes are ornate and fragile; although beautiful, a snowflake would not be suitable for an insignia meant to be worn on the breast or around the neck. But he soon began to come around to the idea.

Staff at the Parliamentary Library copied a number of pages about snowflakes and posted them to Matheson on December 12. Included in each package

RIGHT: A selection of snowflakes taken from the *Encyclopedia Americana*, from the Library of Parliament, as used by John Matheson in 1966. P1b would serve as the model for the Order of Canada insignia shape.

BELOW: Photos from Nakaya's seminal work on snow crystals. The outline of the Order of Canada can be seen in many of these photos.

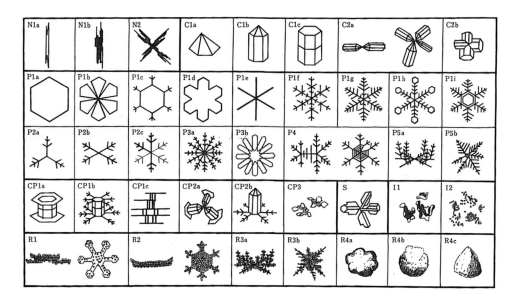

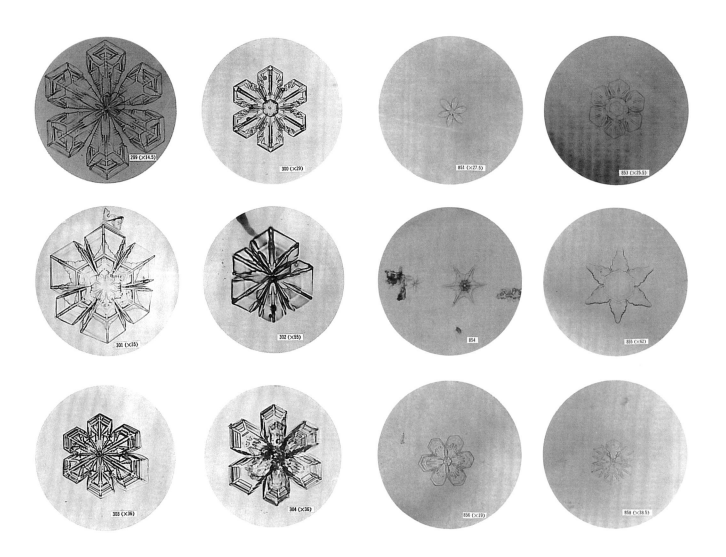

were numerous diagrams and sketches of the various snowflake shapes and the processes by which they form. All snow crystals develop in hexagonal symmetry,[126] so the goal was to design a properly proportioned, elegant yet sturdy snowflake. The diagrams had been taken from Nakaya's seminal work, *Snow Crystals*. The shape chosen was scientifically described as a "Plane Crystal; Crystals developed in the basal plane of the hexagonal system of crystallization … branches in sector form. The branches show the form of tabular sections."[127] This shape served as the model for the Order of Canada insignia.

The symbolism of the snowflake was ideal. It represented the Canadian climate, and furthermore, every snowflake — like every member of the Order — is unique. Prior to Christmas 1966, Beatty submitted three separate designs to the prime minister; Pearson then personally chose the design we have come to know today. The prime minister only commented that the crown appeared a little small and requested that it be enlarged.

Beatty determined that the Companion insignia would measure fifty-six millimetres across, be of white enamel with gold edges, and was to be worn around the neck. In the centre would be a red-enamelled maple leaf surrounded by an annulus in red enamel bearing the motto of the Order in gold letters and four small dots, surmounted by a St. Edward's crown. On the reverse would be the word *Canada* and an inventory number.[128] Made of 18-carat gold, it was a simple yet elegant design. The Medal of Courage and Medal of Service were to be smaller snowflakes — thirty-four millimetres across. These would be worn on the breast like other decorations and medals. The Medal of Courage would be gold in colour, with a simple maple leaf in the centre of the insignia surmounted by a crown. On the reverse would be a circle device containing the word *Courage*. The Medal of Service would be sterling silver, the obverse being identical to the Medal of Courage. On the reverse would be a circle device containing the word *Service*. In both cases, the recipient's name would be engraved on the reverse of the lower arm of the insignia. The prime minister and the governor general approved of the designs; Vanier examined them shortly before his death. The Queen gave approval to the designs on March 21, 1967.[129] The insignia of the Order was now complete, although no actual insignia had yet been manufactured.

In 1972, with the restructuring of the Order of Canada and abolition of the Medal of Courage and Medal of Service, new insignia had to be designed. The Advisory Council determined that the insignia of the two new levels should be scaled-down versions of the very impressive-looking Companion's insignia. This was in part to promote the view that although the Order had three levels, each was a significant part of a broader system of recognition.

The Companion's insignia remained unchanged. The Officer's insignia is nearly identical, except for a few elements to ensure that it can be distinguished from the Companion's. The Officer's insignia is also worn from the neck, but it is only forty-five millimetres across. The obverse is enamelled on a sterling gilt frame, and a single gold maple leaf is located in its centre. The reverse displays the word *Canada* in raised letters with an inventory number impressed below and silver hallmarks on the lower arm. The Member's insignia is worn on the breast and measures thirty-five millimetres across. It is fashioned from silver. The obverse is enamelled, with a silver maple leaf in the centre. The reverse is identical to that of the Officer's insignia.

Miniature Companion, Officer, and Member of the Order of Canada insignia.

There are also the miniature insignia of the Order, which are worn during formal evening functions. These are small, near-exact replicas of the full-size insignia. It has always been the responsibility of the individual member to purchase their own miniature insignia. A number of firms in Britain and Canada have manufactured the miniatures over the years, with there being an active market in old miniatures, which are of much higher quality than the modern products.

Along with the full-size insignia that are presented to each new Companion, Officer, and Member of the Order, recipients are also entitled to wear a lapel badge. This badge takes the form of a small snowflake, displaying in the centre a red, gold, or silver maple leaf, depending on what level of the Order the wearer was appointed to. The practice of wearing a lapel badge or rosette began with France's Légion d'honneur. Recipients wore a small swatch of the ribbon or rosette of the Order on their lapel. When the United States founded its Legion of Merit in 1942, provision was made for wearing a miniature metal version of the badge as a lapel pin. Thus, Canada adopted a blend of French and American traditions.

The idea for an Order of Canada lapel badge was introduced by Sir Conrad Swan. During the development of the Order of Canada, Swan discussed with Prime Minister Pearson the idea of creating special lapel badges for members of the Order. The idea was found to be "highly appropriate and likely to make the Order very acceptable and particularly with French-speaking Canadians."[130] There was the additional advantage that, if recipients of the Order regularly wore their lapel badges, members of the general

LEFT: Miniature Medal of Service of the Order of Canada.

RIGHT: Miniature Medal of Courage of the Order of Canada.

public would be able to recognize not only the Order but also its eminent recipients as having been honoured by the state. This sentiment was echoed by Jack Hodgson, the prime minister's principal secretary, and it was largely at his insistence that the lapel pins were included as part of the Order of Canada.

Though sanctioned in 1967,[131] the lapel badges for members of the Order of Canada were not manufactured and distributed until late 1972.[132] The precise design was developed by Beatty.[133] The reason for the long delay was quite simply that the secretariat of the Order of Canada was too busy dealing with nominations and appointments to be bothered with organizing the logistics of manufacturing and distributing a lapel pin. The first lapel pins were struck in sterling silver and then enamelled.

ABOVE: Grand Officer of the Légion d'honneur lapel badge, which provided the inspiration for the Order of Canada's lapel badges.

LEFT: Companion of the Order of Canada lapel badge.

CENTRE: Officer of the Order of Canada lapel badge.

RIGHT: Member of the Order of Canada lapel badge.

JOHN (JACK) SYNER HODGSON, OBE (1917–1990)

Lester Pearson's principal secretary, Jack Hodgson was a capable public servant who had variously encouraged Diefenbaker and Pearson to consider establishing a national honour. A Rhodes Scholar and holder of a licentiate along with several academic degrees in music, he had risen to the rank of Commander in the Royal Canadian Naval Volunteer Reserve during the Second World War. Hodgson played a role in not only coordinating the establishment of the Order of Canada through the Prime Minister's Office, but also in insisting on the creation of the now-familiar Order of Canada lapel badge that is worn by members of the Order. Hodgson was responsible for many of the arrangements surrounding the early manufacture of the Order. He was also involved with bringing about policies of bilingualism through the Special Secretariat on Bilingualism in the federal government under Pearson. Following Pearson's retirement, Hodgson went on to serve in a number of senior civil service posts.

Companion of the Order of Canada undress ribbon.

Officer of the Order of Canada undress ribbon.

Member of the Order of Canada undress ribbon.

RIGHT: Original sample of the eleven-point maple leaf for the undress ribbons.

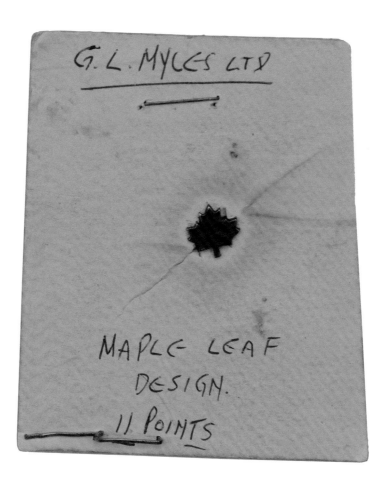

G. L. MYLES LTD

MAPLE LEAF
DESIGN.
11 POINTS

Those who are in uniform do not wear a lapel badge; rather they wear undress ribbons on their various non-combat orders of dress. The undress ribbon consists of a small piece of the full-size ribbon worn on the left breast. In the centre of the ribbon is worn a red, gold, or silver maple leaf, depending on the level of appointment in the Order of Canada held. The original maple leaf devices were designed by Bruce Beatty and procured through the Ottawa tailor shop G.L. Myles. The proper wearing of the lapel badges, full-size insignia, and miniature insignia on appropriate occasions is a way in which individuals display their membership in the Order, but it also helps to publicize the Order.

Each person appointed to the Order of Canada is entitled to use post-nominal initials; this is an old Commonwealth tradition that relates to appointments to orders and the award of decorations only. Since the time of Confederation, use of these post-nominals has become firmly fixed in the Canadian honours landscape. The most universally recognized post-nominal remains VC, for the Victoria Cross. This honour — and its post-nominals — take precedence over all others.

It was only natural that the Order of Canada would carry with it post-nominal initials. When Cabinet agreed to the founding of the Order of Canada with three component parts — consisting of the Companions of the Order, Medal of Courage, and Medal of Service — the post-nominals were set at CC for Companions, CM for holders of the Medal of Courage, and SM for holders of the Medal of Service.[134] MC could not be used for the Medal of Courage as it designated recipients of the Military Cross, a gallantry decoration earned by many Canadians in both world wars and in Korea. Similarly, MS was unacceptable for the Medal of Service because it was already being used in the medical community to designate Master of Surgery. It was no easy task to devise new post-nominals that would not be confused with existing honours, degrees, or qualifications. When the Order was restructured in 1972, the post-nominal initials had to change.

There was no debate about what designation the two new levels should be given. Companions retained the post-nominals CC, the new level of Officer was given the designation OC, and Members were given CM.[135] It is also worth noting that CM was originally intended to be the post-nominal initials accorded to the defunct Canada Medal instituted in 1943.

Along with a full-size insignia and lapel badge, each new member of the Order is presented with an

Companion of the Order of Canada Appointment Scroll.

The Chancellor and Principal Companion of the Order of Canada

Le Chancelier et Compagnon principal de l'Ordre du Canada

To a Colonel the Honourable Sir Leonard C. Outerbridge, Kt., C.B.E., D.S.O., CD

Greeting:

Salut:

Whereas, with the approval of Her Majesty Queen Elizabeth the Second, Sovereign of the Order of Canada, We have been pleased to appoint you to be a Companion of the Order of Canada

We do by these Presents appoint you to be a Companion of the said Order and authorize you to hold and enjoy the dignity of such appointment together with membership in the said Order and all privileges thereunto appertaining

Given at Rideau Hall in the City of Ottawa under the Seal of the Order of Canada this twenty second day of December 1967

By the Chancellor's Command,

Roland Michener

Attendu que, avec l'assentiment de Sa Majesté la Reine Elizabeth Deux, Souveraine de l'Ordre du Canada, il Nous a plu de vous nommer Compagnon de l'Ordre du Canada

Nous vous nommons par les présentes Compagnon dudit Ordre et Nous vous autorisons à bénéficier et à jouir de la dignité de telle nomination ainsi que du titre de membre dudit Ordre et de tous les privilèges y afférents

Fait à Rideau Hall, dans la ville d'Ottawa, sous le Sceau de l'Ordre du Canada, ce vingt deuxième jour de décembre 1967

Par ordre du Chancelier,

Le Secrétaire général de l'Ordre du Canada

Secretary General of the Order of Canada

appointment scroll. The large cream-coloured certificate displays an embossed version the Order of Canada badge at the top in full colour, with the name and post-nominals of the recipient handwritten in calligraphy onto the document by an artist in red gouache ink. Officials at the Chancellery of Honours then place a seal wafer on the bottom of the document where the seal of the Order is impressed. To authenticate the document, it is signed by the secretary general of the Order and the governor general as Chancellor of the Order, on behalf of the Queen.

At the bottom of the scroll is embossed the seal of the Order. Designed by Beatty, the Order's seal is one of the few symbolic elements of the Order of Canada for which we have multiple draft designs — the alternate designs of the insignia having been lost to history after Beatty's death. Three different seal designs were created: all three were circular in shape, circumscribed by the name of the Order in both official languages. The final design was chosen by Roland Michener and was subsequently sent on to the Queen for approval.[136] In his letter petitioning the Queen for acceptance of the seal, Esmond Butler postulated that the seal was "both attractive and heraldically correct."[137] The final design was forwarded on to the Queen for formal approval on June 6, and by June 10, word came that Her Majesty had "signified her approval on the drawing."[138] The Queen then signed the drawing and Prime Minister Pearson subsequently signed the design to signify that the Queen was acting on ministerial advice.[139]

The seal of the Order has a number of applications beyond the appointment scrolls. It is also impressed on all instruments of appointment and all ordinances of the Order — including terminations. A black-and-white image of the seal of the order is also printed at the end of each Order of Canada list published in the *Canada Gazette*. A cameo replica of the Order's seal, made of Tombac (an alloy of 88 percent copper and 12 percent zinc) and measuring 5.5 centimetres in diameter, is presented to each member of the Advisory Council and official of the Order at the end of their mandate or appointment. The edge of each of these is engraved with the name of the recipient.

BELOW LEFT AND CENTRE: Prototype design of the Order of Canada Seal.

BELOW RIGHT: Seal of the Order of Canada as approved by the Queen.

With the establishment of the Canadian Heraldic Authority (CHA) in 1988, the motto circlet of the Order and its insignia have frequently been displayed in Canadian grants of arms. In heraldry it has been the tradition for holders of senior honours to have their insignia depicted with their arms; this has been the case in most European heraldic traditions.[140] The practice of displaying the insignia of honours with coats of arms can be traced back to the early fifteenth century, shortly after the establishment of the Order of the Garter. Knights of the Garter would often encircle the shield of their arms with the motto of the Order inscribed in gold on a blue garter with a gold buckle, and by the reign of Henry VII (1485–1509) this had become common practice.

It was only in the early nineteenth century that it became common practice for the insignia of orders to be hung from the shield of a person's coat of arms. In more recent times, it has been customary for the holders of the higher levels of the imperial orders of chivalry (knights and dames, companions and commanders) to surround their shield with the circlet bearing the motto of the order to which they belong. Officers and members of the various imperial orders are not entitled to use a motto circlet.

The system adopted by the CHA in relation to Canadian honours has been far more inclusive. All members of the three Canadian state orders (the Order of Canada, the Order of Military Merit, and the Order of Merit of the Police Forces) may include the motto circlet of their particular order, regardless of their level of membership.

Members of the Order of Canada, many of whom have petitioned for arms from the CHA, will invariably be granted arms that include the motto circlet of the Order of Canada, displaying the full motto in gold, and include the insignia of their level of membership — Companion, Officer, or Member — along with the potential for including depictions of the insignia of two other honours of the Crown. Companions of the Order of Canada are also entitled to supporters (figures that stand on each side of the shield to support it).

Left: The arms of Colonel the Honourable Donald Ethell, OC, OMM, AOE, MSC, CD.

Right: The arms of the Honourable Sylvia Olga Fedoruk, OC, SOM.

LEFT: The Right Honourable Paul
Martin, PC, CC.

RIGHT: The arms of Sir Christopher
Ondaatje, OC, CBE.

LEFT: The arms of John C. Perlin,
CM, CVO, ONL.

RIGHT: The arms of Douglas Graeme
Bassett, OC, OOnt.

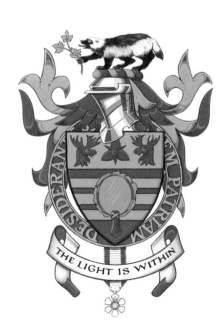

LEFT: The arms of Young Sup
Chung, CM, CQ.

RIGHT: The arms of Dean
Cameron, CM.

ELEVEN

CRAFTING A
TOKEN OF RECOGNITION:
MANUFACTURING THE INSIGNIA

The outward symbol of the Order of Canada is the insignia that every member is invested with. These beautifully crafted tokens of recognition conferred by the Crown are stunning examples of a rare craft, requiring the precision of an engineer and the finesse of a court jeweller.

With fewer than two hundred people appointed to the Order annually, the insignia are made as required, usually twice a year, several months in advance of each investiture. Each insignia is made up of multiple pieces and is handcrafted and numbered. The manufacture of the Order's insignia is a complex process that requires the detailed work of many talented artisans. While Bruce Beatty designed the insignia, the job of developing the technical designs and drawings was initially undertaken by William Summers, the Crown Jeweller who worked for Garrard & Company in London, UK, which produced the original insignia. When the manufacture was transferred to a Canadian manufacturer in 1984, the government had a new set of dies made for the striking of the various components that make up the insignia. The steps and process outlined herein are those used from 1984 to 2015, and would have been very similar to those used by Garrard & Company from 1967 to 1984. The images are of the Order of Military Merit being crafted. Details and images of the process presently used by the Royal Canadian Mint were unavailable.

1–4.   The process starts by rolling the material, in this case sterling silver, to the appropriate thickness and striking out blanks in the general shape of the insignia. Each component is struck separately; the snowflake

Steps 1–4

(two dies, front and back), the motto circlet and crown, the central maple leaf, the reverse centre cap, and, for the Officer and Companion levels, there is the suspender through which the ribbon passes — this is also called the bail.

5. The dies are set in a hydraulic press.

6. A blank is placed between the two dies for the component and struck to impress the design on both sides.

7. Only one die is used for one-sided pieces such as the reverse cap, motto circlet, and maple leaf.

BELOW: Step 5
BELOW RIGHT: Steps 6–7

8. Each piece is struck between two and four times under up to 175 tons of pressure, and the piece is annealed in a furnace between each strike.

9. Each piece is then cut to remove the excess material and finished by hand.

10–11. The enamel powder is mixed with a little water to make the application easier. Each field created by raised edges in the striking process is filled with wet enamel paste of the appropriate colour.

12–13. Once the enamel powder has dried in place, the piece is fired in a kiln at an average of 900 degrees Celsius, so that the enamel powder liquefies and then solidifies upon cooling to form the vitreous enamel in the specified shade.

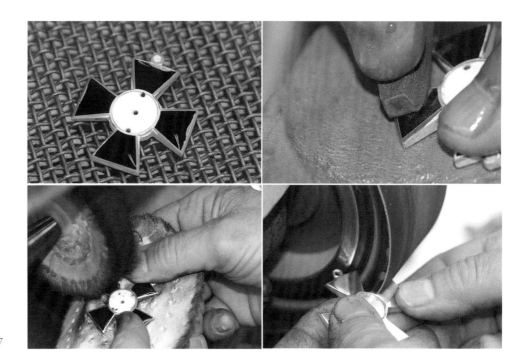

Steps 14–17

14–16. The enamel has to be built up in consecutive layers and fired between each application until the enamel protrudes over the raised edge of the field. Any imperfections have to be picked out at every stage and any air bubbles that form may result in the enamel popping during firing. The enamel is then ground down (15) and polished to a smooth finish using a range of increasingly finer files and polishing stones.

17. The metal parts are then buffed and polished.

18. The enamelled pieces for the insignia of Companion and Officer are then plated in 24-carat gold; those for the Member insignia remain silver in colour. The various components are then assembled together by riveting posts into drilled holes.

19–20. The centre maple leaf is affixed to the snowflake (20), followed by the circlet and crown (21), then the back is covered with the reverse cap bearing the insignia number.

21. The insignia is cleaned and is now ready to be mounted with its distinctive red-and-white ribbon; ready for presentation by the governor general.

Steps 19–21

Companion Medal

- Sterling Silver 65 dwt (approximate)
- 24K Gold Plating
- SawCut/Pierced, 6 Pieces
- Loop and Bale
- Red/B/ue/White Enamel
- 2 Ruby, 2 Emerald, 1 Sapphire in Crown
- Polished Front, Polished Back
- Sequential Die Struck Numbers on Back
- Plastic Bag

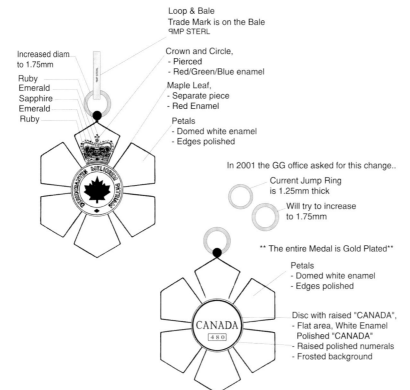

Loop & Bale
Trade Mark is on the Bale
9MP STERL

Increased diam
to 1.75mm

Ruby
Emerald
Sapphire
Emerald
Ruby

Crown and Circle,
- Pierced
- Red/Green/Blue enamel

Maple Leaf,
- Separate piece
- Red Enamel

Petals
- Domed white enamel
- Edges polished

In 2001 the GG office asked for this change..

Current Jump Ring
is 1.25mm thick

Will try to increase
to 1.75mm

** The entire Medal is Gold Plated**

Petals
- Domed white enamel
- Edges polished

CANADA
480

Disc with raised "CANADA",
- Flat area, White Enamel
  Polished "CANADA"
- Raised polished numerals
- Frosted background

Technical drawings for the
Order of Canada from Pressed
Metal Products.

* * *

From 1967 to 2015 the Order of Canada insignia was manufactured by a variety of firms, beginning with Garrard & Company of London. Rideau Ltée was the first Canadian company to produce the insignia; they were followed by Pressed Metal Products and Bond Boyd Ltd. In 2015 production of the insignia of the Order was transferred to the Royal Canadian Mint. This resulted in several changes, notably the metal from which the insignia is struck is now .9999 silver as opposed to .925 sterling silver. The reverse cap is no longer a separate piece; the ring suspension for the CM is now a separate piece as opposed to being one with the snowflake frame as before; and in place of vitreous enamel (glass), the white and red elements of the insignia are now filled with an epoxy resin fill (plastic). The small lapel badges of the Order are crafted in a similar fashion and are usually posted to a newly appointed recipient shortly after their appointment is announced so that they can immediately begin wearing it.

LEFT: Companion of the Order of Canada, first Garrard issue with large maple leaf.

RIGHT: Companion of the Order of Canada, second Garrard issue with small maple leaf.

LEFT: Companion of the Order of Canada, Pressed Metal Products issue. Small diamond replaced four dots at base of motto circlet, and shape of jewels became round.

RIGHT: Companion of the Order of Canada, Royal Canadian Mint issue, with epoxy fill in place of vitreous enamel.

Top row, left: Officer of the Order of Canada, Pressed Medal Products issue.
Top row, centre: Officer of the Order of Canada, Garrard issue.
Top row, right: Officer of the Order of Canada, Garrard reverse; note sterling hallmarks.

Middle row, left: Member of the Order of Canada, Garrard issue.
Middle row, right: Member of the Order of Canada, Pressed Metal Products issue.

Bottom row, left: Member of the Order of Canada, Royal Canadian Mint issue.
Bottom row, right: Member of the Order of Canada, reverse, Birks issue.

MANUFACTURERS OF THE ORDER OF CANADA INSIGNIA

Manufacturer	Companion	Officer & Member
Garrard & Co	**Marks:** Un-hallmarked **Location:** Reverse of the hanger (rare) **Material:** 18-carat gold **Dates:** 1967–84	**Marks:** "G&Co" and usual British hallmarks **Location:** Reverse of the lower arm **Material:** .925 silver (gold-plated for OC) **Other:** Some early OC issues carry no hallmarks; in 1978 a small number were marked "SILVER" in place of "G&Co" **Dates:** 1972–83
Rideau Ltée	**Marks:** Early insignia unmarked; post-2004 insignia are laser engraved with "RIDEAU + R STER" **Location:** hanger or reverse of mounting ball or the edge of the lowest arm **Material:** 18-carat gold from 1984–1996, thereafter .925 silver gold plated **Dates:** 1985–96, 2004–05	**Marks:** "RIDEAU + R STER" **Location:** Reverse of the lower arm **Material:** .925 silver (gold plated for OC) **Dates for OC:** 1983–96, 2004–05 **Dates for CM:** 1983–96, 2004–05, 2008–09, 2012
Birks (Pressed Metal Products)	**Marks:** "BIRKS STER" **Location:** Reverse of the hanger **Material:** .925 silver gold plated **Dates:** 1996–2004, 2006–11	**Marks:** "BIRKS STER" **Location:** Reverse of the lower arm **Material:** .925 silver (gold plated for OC) **Dates for OC:** 1996–2004, 2006–07 **Dates for CM:** 1998–2004, 2006–07
Pressed Metal Products	**Marks:** "PMP STER" **Location:** Reverse of the hanger **Material:** .925 silver gold plated **Dates:** 2011	**Marks:** "PMP STER" **Location:** Reverse of the lower arm **Material:** .925 silver (gold plated for OC) **Dates:** 2010–13
Bond Boyd Ltd	**N/A**	**Marks:** "BOND BOYD STER" **Location:** Reverse of the lower arm **Material:** .925 silver (gold plated for OC) **Dates:** 2010
Royal Canadian Mint	**Marks:** RCM logo on reverse of hanger **Location:** Reverse of the hanger **Material:** .999 silver **Dates:** 2014–	**Marks:** RCM logo **Location:** Reverse of the lower arm **Material:** .999 silver (gold plated for OC) **Dates:** 2014–

TWELVE

CENTREPIECE OF AN
HONOURS SYSTEM

For fifty years, the Order of Canada has sought to recognize outstanding Canadians who have made lasting contributions on the local, national, and international stages. The establishment of the Order and the broader Canadian honours system took elements from the British and French honours systems; however, the grassroots-based, non-partisan model developed as a direct result of the Nickle Debates of 1917–19 and Canadian opposition to patronage-based honours. R.B. Bennett's groundbreaking decision to use civil honours to recognize men and women from all regions of the country, and based entirely on merit, was a transition point in the history of honours in Canada.

Eschewing the old patronage-based model for one based on greater equality, and recognition of non-traditional fields and those involved in work at the community level, helped to demonstrate how honours could be used to recognize exemplary citizenship at all levels of society.

Like the national flag of Canada and the Royal Commission on Bilingualism and Biculturalism, the Order of Canada was created out of a sense of urgency and was seen as another mechanism to help enhance the unity of the country. The development of a uniquely Canadian honours system, made up of Canadian symbols, also coincided

A pair of Companion's insignia.

Top: Expo 67, Montreal.

Above: 1967 Centennial logo.

with the broader realization that Canada was an independent actor on the international stage; we were no longer a dependent of the United Kingdom. It was also a tidy addition to the broader project of enhancing the Canadian character of the Crown, thereby more fully Canadianizing a core institution of government and civil society.

The establishment of the Order of Canada flowed from the preparations for the 1967 Centennial celebrations, and the energy that surrounded marquee events such as Expo 67. Those involved in the creation of the Order were aware that they were engaging in the "invention of tradition," and there was no attempt to cloak the new institution in a mock ancient ceremony or link it to some previous event. Creating a new tradition and process, employing familiar symbols but with various innovations, was necessary if the new institution was to gain support — or at least not arouse opposition — from all corners of the country.

The success of the Order can be seen not only in the contributions of the more than six thousand people appointed to the Order since 1967, but by the fact that each province, and even far-off places, such as Australia, have modelled their various orders on the template pioneered by the Order of Canada.

The Order is a living institution, defined by the membership of the Order and also by those who dutifully and carefully administer its operation. The desire to

DR. HENRY MORGENTALER
HONOURED

Canada's
ABORTION
DEBATE

MACKAY
HAMILTON SPECTATOR

LEFT: Cartoon by Mackay of the *Hamilton Spectator*, published following the appointment of Dr. Henry Morgentaler as a Member of the Order, 2008.

BELOW: Cartoon, by Patrick Corrigan of the *Toronto Star*, commenting on the distribution of the Order of Canada.

recognize exemplary citizenship in all of its forms, as exemplified by the Order's motto — *Desiderantes meliorem patriam* — continues to be a touchstone of what it means to be a Canadian. While the face of the Order's membership has greatly diversified since 1967, as has the population of the country, the constant goal of recognizing those who enhance our communities, large and small, is what helps to give the Order legitimacy and purpose beyond simply a bit of tinsel hung from a piece of silk.

It would be naive to suggest that every appointment has met with universal approval, and in retrospect one can discern a few ill-advised ones; yet this is perhaps inevitable, and does not detract from the overall impact of the Order. Like all great national institutions,

PEANUTS...
POPCORN...
ORDER OF
CANADA...

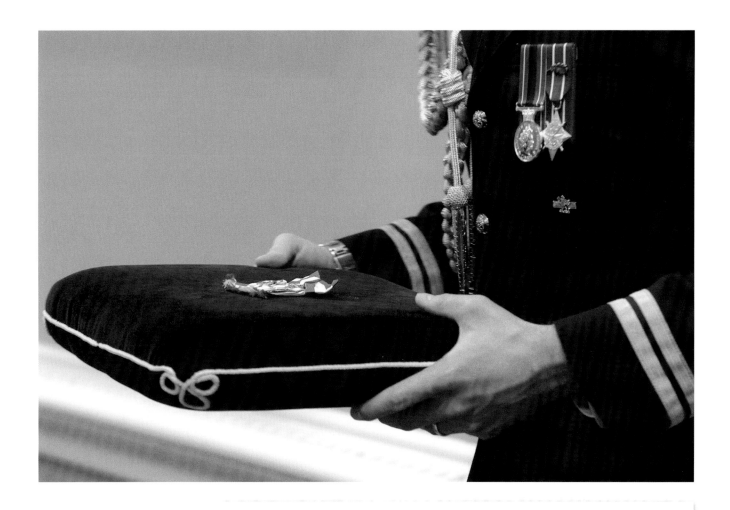

The Governor General of Canada
Chancellor and Principal Companion
of the Order of Canada

Le gouverneur général du Canada
chancelier et compagnon principal
de l'Ordre du Canada

to   à

Janet Rossant, C.C.

Greeting :   Salut :

Whereas, with the approval of Her Majesty Queen Elizabeth the Second, Sovereign of the Order of Canada, We have been pleased to appoint you to the Order of Canada

Attendu que, avec l'assentiment de Sa Majesté la reine Elizabeth Deux, souveraine de l'Ordre du Canada, il Nous a plu de vous nommer à l'Ordre du Canada

We do by these Presents appoint you to be a Companion of the said Order and authorize you to hold and enjoy the dignity of such appointment together with membership in the said Order and all privileges thereunto appertaining

Nous vous nommons par les présentes Compagnon dudit Ordre et Nous vous autorisons à bénéficier et à jouir de la dignité de telle nomination ainsi que du titre de membre dudit Ordre et de tous les privilèges y afférents

Given at Rideau Hall in the City of Ottawa under the Seal of the Order of Canada this 7th day of May, 2015

Fait à Rideau Hall dans la ville d'Ottawa, sous le Sceau de l'Ordre du Canada, ce 7e jour de mai 2015

By the Chancellor's Command,

Par ordre du chancelier,

Le secrétaire général de l'Ordre du Canada

Secretary General of the Order of Canada

RIGHT: Modern Order of Canada
appointment scroll.

the Order has not been without controversy. The removal of disgraced hockey czar Alan Eagleson and the embezzling arts promoter Garth Drabinsky and the failure to remove ignominious sports figures such as Ben Johnson and Angella Taylor-Issajenko, has added a sense of drama and reality to an overwhelmingly exemplary society of honour. Similarly, the 2008 appointment of Dr. Henry Morgentaler, the abortion rights crusader, celebrated by his supporters and reviled by his detractors, brought discussion about the Order and its appointment process to every newscast and the front pages of every newspaper. Nevertheless, of the six thousand members of the Order, one is hard-pressed to find more than a few dozen whose appointment or refusal has caused great public discourse or outcry.

The ultimate expression of the Order's legitimacy is the calibre of those who have joined its ranks. Canadians from every corner of our country and every walk of life have been admitted to the Order by virtue of their contributions. We will not soon forget the likes of Charles Best, Ursula Franklin, Pauline McGibbon, Jean Drapeau, Cardinal Léger, Eugene Forsey, Yousuf Karsh, Evelyn Cudmore, or Terry Fox, all of whom belonged to the Order. Their stories are but a single page out of the Order's register, yet they speak volumes about Canada's recent history.

That the Order's establishment also helped to spawn the creation of the broader Canadian honours system, which has to date recognized more than 350,000 people across the country, is another important aspect of the influence it has had. Today, Canada has one of the most extensive, accessible, and equitable honours systems in the world, driven by grassroots nominations, a non-partisan selection process, and the desire to recognize citizens from all regions and walks of life. When one reflects on the public perception of civil honours that existed following the end of the First World War — as a patronage-riddled system that enhanced class differentiations — one gains a more precise understanding of how far our

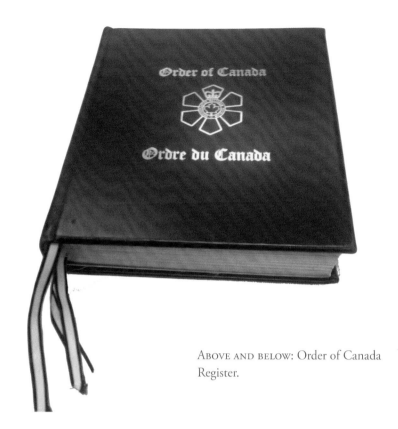

ABOVE AND BELOW: Order of Canada Register.

honours system has come over the past century. That Canada went nearly fifty years with no civilian honours system also speaks to the fragility even a widely accepted and respected institution can have if not nurtured and tended.

The now-familiar white snowflake has become widely viewed as a particular mark of distinction and merit. The acceptance and high regard for the Order, and the Canadian honours system as a whole, has taken time to mature and fully develop. The story of the Order's growth and evolution over the past fifty years encapsulates many aspects of the changes Canada has undergone over the same period — the two being intimately connected. To understand the builders of Canada in modern times, one must become familiar with those who have populated the Order's membership.

The society of honour established at the insistence of Lester B. Pearson and devised by Vincent Massey, Esmond Butler, Gordon Robertson, Jack Hodgson, Michael Pitfield, John Matheson, and other members of the baker's dozen who were deeply involved in the Order's creation, is the most equitable and fair system yet devised. How far we have come from the age of W.F. Nickle, who is in many ways the father of our concept of what honours should embody. His disdain for partisan patronage, flunkeyism, and social gradation served as a catalyst for the nearly half-century-long project to create a Canadian Order.

If snowflakes are indeed letters from heaven, to paraphrase Ukichiro Nakaya, then one can look upon those who have been recognized with the Order's familiar snowflake as individual gifts to the people of Canada and the world.

Left: Bronze paperweights have been presented to Members of the Advisory Council at the conclusion of their service on the council.

Right: Two special strikings were made in silver recovered from the melting of the returned Medals of Service of the Order of Canada in 1984.

ACKNOWLEDGEMENTS

Writing this book was relatively easy, given that I commenced working on it shortly after the second edition of *The Canadian Honours System* went off to press. I am grateful to the usual cadre of colleagues and friends who support my various writing endeavours. As always, thanks are owed to Lieutenant-Colonel Carl Gauthier for editing this manuscript and for introducing me to the French book, *De Gaulle et le Mérite: Création d'un ordre républicain*, which served as an inspiration for this work. Gratitude is owed to Matthew Malone who survived this project without complaint.

I am also grateful to Joyce Bryant, the first employee of the Order of Canada secretariat and herself a Member of the Order. For nearly fifteen years, she has been a constant source of encouragement and guidance. Having the internationally renowned humanitarian Jean Vanier provide the foreword to this work is a great honour. A man who epitomizes the motto of the Order, Vanier, like his distinguished parents, has done so much to enhance the lives of others.

I remain indebted to Dundurn Press and its president, Kirk Howard, for their ongoing support and publishing of my work. Without the unwavering encouragement of Dundurn, it is unlikely I would have ever published a single book, let alone a dozen.

A more ubiquitous thank you is owed to the hundreds of members of the Order of Canada whom I have come to know over the past two decades. Their example, encouragement, and interest in my work have more than made up for the persistent lack of interest in our honours system shown by so many officials over the same period.

Christopher McCreery, MVO
Government House
Halifax

NOTES

1. Samuel Clark, *Distributing Status* (Montreal: McGill-Queen's University Press, 2016), 345.
2. Library and Archives Canada (LAC), MG 26 J1, Mackenzie King Papers, 396,117, Lord Alexander to Mackenzie King, March 24, 1948.
3. LAC, MG 26 J1, Mackenzie King Papers, 396,120, Lord Alexander to Mackenzie King, March 24, 1948.
4. LAC, MG 26 J1, Mackenzie King Papers, 396,117, Lord Alexander to Mackenzie King, March 24, 1948.
5. LAC, RG 24, vol. 7019, Resolution of the Conference of Defence Associations, January 30, 1960.
6. LAC, RG 24, 2802, vol. 4, 24,538, Brief on the Order of Canada for the Consideration of the Chiefs of Staff Committee, submitted by the Personnel Members Committee, February 26, 1960.
7. LAC, RG 24, 2802, vol. 4, 24,538, Minutes of a Meeting of the Government Decorations Committee, March 11, 1960.
8. Ibid.
9. LAC, RG 24, 2802, vol. 4, 24,538, Mrs. Anne Corbett to Brigadier T.A. Johnston, March 21, 1960. Also confirmed in interview with Michael Hodgson, son of John (Jack) Hodgson, November 17, 2005. Hodgson recounted his father's story of Diefenbaker's negative reaction when he suggested establishing an Order of Canada in 1959.

10. LAC, MG 31 E80, vol. 7, Butler Papers, Memorandum from Butler to Vanier, February 15, 1961. Also interview with Michael Hodgson, November 17, 2005.

11. LAC, R 5769, vol. 11, Lochnan Papers, Memorandum for Carl Lochnan from Esmond Butler, March 19, 1976.

12. DND/DHH, 75/506, Centennial Medal. On June 28, 1962, the Personnel Members Committee proposed the creation of a Centennial Medal "to commemorate Canada's 100th anniversary." For a complete history of commemorative medals, see Christopher McCreery, *Commemorative Medals of The Queen's Reign in Canada, 1952–2012* (Toronto: Dundurn Press, 2012).

13. LAC, RG 2, Cabinet Submission from Paul Hellyer and Maurice Lamontagne, May 11, 1965.

14. LAC, R 5769, vol. 12, file 16, Lochnan Papers., O.G. Stoner (Privy Council Office staff) to Jean Miquelon (chairman of the Decorations Committee), September 30, 1965.

15. Matheson spoke with Pearson about the matter in 1962. Matheson Interview, August 24, 2001.

16. Lester B. Pearson, *Mike: The Memoirs of the Rt. Hon Lester B. Pearson,* vol. 2 (Toronto: University of Toronto Press, 1973), 302.

17. Pearson received his OBE over the fence of a tennis court in 1935. Pearson, 302.

18. Pearson recalling his reaction to the 1943 honours list. Pearson, 302.

19. John English, *The Worldly Years: The Life of Lester Pearson* (Toronto: Vintage Books, 1993), 140.

20. West Sussex Country Records Office, Bessborough Papers, Bessborough to King George V, December 18, 1934.

21. The maple leaf was used on the coins issued by New Brunswick, Nova Scotia, and the Province of Canada prior to Confederation, and used on the first Dominion coinage issued from 1876 to 1936. *The Charlton Standard Catalogue of Canadian Coins* (Toronto: Charlton Press, 2001).

22. John R. Matheson, *Canada's Flag : A Search for a Country* (Boston: G.K. Hall Press, 1980), 122.

23. Ibid., 122.

24. Lester B. Pearson, *Mike: the Memoirs of the Rt. Hon. Lester B. Pearson* (Toronto: University of Toronto Press, 1975), vol. 3, 274.

25. Ibid., 281.

26. House of Commons, *Debates*, November 6, 1963, 4449.

27. Bill C-92, House of Commons, April 8, 1965 (Ottawa: Queen's Printer, 1965).

28. Pearson, *Mike*, vol. 3, 210.

29. University of Toronto Archives (UTA), Massey Papers, Vincent Massey to Lester Pearson, February 3, 1966.

30. Ibid.

31. Ibid., Lester Pearson to Vincent Massey, February 17, 1966.

32. Ibid., Vincent Massey to Lester Pearson, March 9, 1966.

33. Near Port Hope, Ontario.

34. UTA, Massey Papers, Vincent Massey to Esmond Butler, March 14, 1966.

35. Massey set about drawing up a constitution for the Order. Although the first draft was not completed until March 23, many of the details were agreed to during Matheson's visit of March 16–17. UTA, Massey Papers, March 23, 1966, Proposal for a Canadian Order.

36. The meeting between Pearson and Vanier occurred on the evening of March 17. UTA, Massey Papers, Esmond Butler to Vincent Massey, March 18, 1966.

37. LAC, MG 32 A2, vol. 24, file 9, Georges Vanier Papers, Esmond Butler to Vincent Massey, March 18, 1966. The fact that this letter (also found in the Massey and Butler Papers) is located in the Vanier Papers indicated that Vanier was aware of the project from the earliest stage. Unfortunately, there is no record of his conversation with Pearson on March 18, 1966.

38. Ibid.

39. Ibid.

40. LAC, R 5769, vol. 12, Lochnan Papers, Historical Report, 1986.

41. Queen's University Archives (QUA), Matheson Papers, file 295, Esmond Butler to John Matheson, March 31, 1966.

42. Ibid.

43. Ibid.

44. Although Pitfield did not outline that each of the three types of Canada Medals were to be different, it would only be logical that they were intended as such. This was further discussed by John Matheson and Conrad Swan on April 25, 1966, and can be found in QUA, Matheson Papers, file 295, John Matheson to Lester Pearson, April 29, 1966.

45. Ibid., April 14, 1966. Also see LAC, MG 26 N4, vol. 1, file 001-42.

46. LAC, MG 26 N4, vol. 1, file 001-42, John Matheson to Lester Pearson, April 14, 1966, notes in Pearson's handwriting on document not found on copy in Matheson Papers.

47. UTA, Massey Papers, Esmond Butler to Vincent Massey, July 25, 1966.

48. LAC, MG 31 E80, vol. 7, file 8, Butler Papers, Esmond Butler to Georges Vanier, May 6, 1966.

49. LAC, MG 32 A2, vol. 33, Vincent Massey to Georges Vanier, July 12, 1966.

50. Ibid., Georges Vanier to Vincent Massey, July 29, 1966.

51. UTA, Massey Papers, Esmond Butler to Vincent Massey, August 26, 1966.

52. LAC, MG 26 N4, vol. 1, file 001-4, Pearson Papers, Vincent Massey to Lester Pearson, September 28, 1966.

53. Ibid., Lester Pearson to Vincent Massey, October 3, 1966.

54. QUA, file 296, Matheson Papers, John Matheson to Mary Macdonald, September 1966.

55. Ibid., Cabinet Document 625-66, November 7, 1966.

56. LAC RG 2, Cabinet Document 625-66, November 7, 1966.

57. Chancellery of Honours (CHAN), Black Binder, Secret Memorandum from Pitfield to Butler, Hodgson, and Matheson, November 25, 1966. Pitfield acknowledged that some change in the Advisory Council was necessary "so that it would not be dominated by persons close to the federal government."

58. LAC, RG 2, vol. 6321, Cabinet Conclusions No. 136-66, November 29, 1966.

59. This was a revised version of the October 19 Constitution.

60. CHAN, Black Binder, Adeane to Butler, January 10, 1967. LAC, R 5769, Lochnan Papers, vol. 12.

61. LAC, MG 26 N4, vol. 1, file 001-42, Pearson Papers, Sir Michael Adeane to Esmond Butler, January 9, 1967.

62. Ibid., Esmond Butler to Sir Michael Adeane, January 13, 1967.

63. CHAN, Black Binder, Memorandum from Hodgson to Matheson, Butler, and Pitfield, December 21, 1966. LAC, R 5769, Lochnan Papers, vol. 12.

64. QUA, Matheson Papers, file 225, Constitution of the Order of Canada, February 1967.

65. It is unclear whether the Canadian government planned on continuing to use the Victoria Cross and George Cross. For a full discussion of Canadian appointments to the Order of the British Empire for gallantry, see *The Order of Military Merit* (Ottawa: Department of National Defence, 2012), 47–51.

66. CHAN, Black Binder, Esmond Butler to Georges Vanier, February 17, 1967. LAC, R 5769, Lochnan Papers, vol. 12.

67. Constitution of the Order of Canada, 1967.

68. LAC, RG 2, vol. 6323, file 20-67, Cabinet Conclusions, March 2, 1967.

69. Ibid., Sir Michael Adeane to Georges Vanier, February 27, 1967. LAC, R 5769, vol. 12, Lochnan Papers.

70. LAC, R 5967, vol. 12, Lochnan Papers, Gordon Robertson to Judy LaMarsh, March 13, 1967.

71. Ibid.

72. CHAN, Black Binder, Assistant Secretary to the Governor General to the Private Secretary to the Queen, March 17, 1967.

73. LAC, MG 26 N4, vol. 1, file 001-42, John Hodgson to Lester Pearson, March 23, 1967.

74. House of Commons, *Debates*, April 17, 1967, 14,968 (Pearson).

75. Ibid., 14,969 (Diefenbaker).

76. Ibid., 14,969 (David Lewis).

77. Gary Miedema, *For Canada's Sake: Public Religion, Centennial Celebrations, and the Re-making of Canada in the 1960s* (Montreal: McGill-Queen's University Press, 2005), 146.

78. LAC, RG 2, vol. 6323, file 20-67, Cabinet Conclusions, March 2, 1967. Cabinet approved and passed Order-in-Council 388 that revoked the Order-in-Council that founded the Canada Medal.

79. QUA, Matheson Papers, Series 2, File 224, GG Remarks at Joint Luncheon for the Kiwanis and Rotary Clubs, Macdonald Hotel, Edmonton, November 7, 1967.

80. UTA, Massey Papers, Resolution of the Royal Society of Canada, 1951.

81. Interview with Gordon Robertson, December 6, 2001.

82. Esmond Butler's introductory address to the Advisory Council of the Order of Canada, May 29, 1967. Taken from Butler's speech for the special meeting of the Advisory Council of the Order of Canada, January 17, 1977. LAC, R 5769, vol. 10, file 22, Lochnan Papers.

83. LAC, R 5769, vol. 11, Lochnan Papers, Memorandum: Procedures Relative to Appointment of Nominees, March 13, 1975.

84. LAC, MG 32 B41, vol. 134, Sharp Papers, Roland Michener to Mitchell Sharp, December 14, 1967.

85. Ibid.

86. Ibid.

87. Interview with Gordon Robertson, December 6, 2001.

88. Cabinet Office Ceremonial Secretariat [COCS] C135, "Canadian Attitudes to Imperial Honours, 1943–1967," Esmond Butler to Sir Michael Adeane, April 20, 1972.

89. LAC, R 5769, vol. 11, Lochnan Papers, Carl Lochnan to G.G.E. Steele, October 26, 1968.

90. This proposal was first devised on October 28, 1968, at the meeting of the subcommittee of the Government Decorations Committee.

91. Order of Canada citation for HRH the Duke of Edinburgh.

92. LAC, R 5769, vol. 11, Lochnan Papers, Minutes of a meeting with His Excellency, August 23, 1967.

93. Order of Canada citation for Terry Fox, CC.

94. CBC television interview with Terry Fox, September 19, 1980.

95. The 125th Anniversary of Confederation Medal was designed by Bruce Beatty.

96. CHAN, Speech on the Occasion of the Order of Canada Investiture, October 21, 1992.

97. CHAN, Speech on the Occasion of the Order of Canada Investiture, October 26, 2007.

98. Order of Canada citation for Joyce Bryant, CM, BEM, December 17, 1973.

99. Joyce Bryant, *Slender Threads* (Lifewriters Press, 2007), 1.

100. Ibid., 2.

101. Order of Canada citation for Esmond Unwin Butler, CVO, OC.

102. Interview with Bruce Beatty, September 3, 2002.

103. Order of Canada citation for Bruce W. Beatty, CM, SOM, CD.

104. QUA, Matheson Papers, file 226, Matheson Notes on Honours, March/April 1966.

105. Joyce Turpin (later Bryant), Vincent Massey's secretary, suggested that the name of the Order be the Order of the Cross of Canada. UTA, Massey Papers, vol. 363, Notes for Mr. Massey from Joyce Turpin, March 25, 1966.

106. LAC, R 5769, vol. 11, Lochnan Papers, Memorandum from Michael Pitfield to Esmond Butler and John Matheson, April 13, 1966.

107. Sir Conrad Swan, *A King from Canada* (London: Memoir Club, 2005), 220.

108. LAC, RG 24, vol. 4059, file 1078-14-5, Memorandum from A. Fortescue Duguid to H.F.G. Letson, March 29, 1943.

109. QUA, Matheson Papers, file 295, Philip Laundy to John Matheson, February 10, 1966.

110. QUA, Matheson Papers, file 295, Herbert O'Driscoll, Notes on speech to the Seminar on International Affairs, 1966.

111. Ibid.

112. QUA, Matheson Papers, file 226, Rough Notes, March 1966. These notes contain the first reference to the motto "Desires a better country," and comprise part of Matheson's early research. They date at roughly the same time that Matheson had commissioned the Parliamentary Library to research honours for him. Also see QUA, Matheson Papers, Philip Laundy to John Matheson, February 10, 1966. Matheson interview, January 7, 2000.

113. LAC, MG 26 N4, vol. 1, file 001-42, Pearson Papers. Philip Laundy to Jack Hodgson, October 3, 1966.

114. An early version of the Order's constitution is marked with the incorrect passage number 12:16, CHAN 708-3 file 1.

115. *Toronto Daily Star*, April 18, 1967. Also see the Toronto *Globe and Mail*, April 18, 1967.

116. LAC, RG 2, vol. 80, H-5, Honours and Decorations, 1945.

117. LAC, RG 2, vol. 9, H-5, May 3, 1943, Proposal for the Canadian Decoration of Honour.

118. QUA, Matheson Papers, file 227, A Proposal for the Establishment of the Order of Canada, April 1966.

119. A remnant of this proposed sash can be found in the Massey Papers at the University of Toronto Archives.

120. LAC, MH 26 N4, vol. 1, file 001-42, Pearson Papers, John Matheson to Lester Pearson, July 14, 1966.

121. LAC, RG 2, vol. 80, file H-5, 1943 and 1945, Proposal for the Order of Canada.

122. Ibid., May 3, 1943, Proposal for the Canadian Award of Honour and Canadian Decoration of Honour.

123. Ibid., March 28, 1966.

124. QUA, Matheson Papers, file 314, John Matheson to Lester Pearson, November 21, 1966. Although Matheson makes no mention of his discussion with Halstead, this is the only occasion when the two men had contact with each other between November and December 1966, when the snowflake design was chosen as the basis for the Order of Canada.

125. Interview with John R. Matheson, October 2, 2001. Matheson quoting John Halstead. Also see LAC, R 974, vol. 21, Halstead Papers, Eulogy to Halstead by Jake Warren, 1998.

126. Ukichiro Nakaya, *Snow Crystals: Natural and Artificial* (Cambridge: Harvard University Press, 1954), 1.

127. Nakaya, *Snow Crystals*, 80, 86.

128. Although the three-digit number on the reverse of the Companion's insignia was originally intended merely as a method of inventory tracking (i.e., stock numbers) a register of the numbers has been maintained by the Chancellery, and today one can identify the recipient of a particular insignia (Companion, Officer, or Member) by looking up a particular number in the register. Companion's insignia started with number 01, while those of Officer and Member started with 1.

129. LAC, MG 26 N4, vol. 1, file 001-42, John Hodgson to Lester Pearson, March 23, 1967.

130. LAC, MG 26 N4, vol. 1, file 001-42, Pearson Papers, Sir Conrad Swan to John Hodgson, September 28, 1966. Also discussed during Pearson's visit to London, September 1966.

131. LAC, R 5769, vol. 11, Lochnan Papers, Minutes of a Meeting with His Excellency the governor general, August 23, 1967.

132. At a meeting on February 25, 1972, the governor general was wondering why the lapel badges had not yet been prepared. CHAN 600-0 Order of Canada Procedures, Memorandum for Mr. Butler from Roger de C. Nantel, February 29, 1972.

133. LAC, MG 26 N4, vol. 1, file 001-42, Pearson Papers, Conrad Swan to John Hodgson, September 28, 1966. Also discussed during Pearson's visit to London, September 1966.

134. LAC, MG 26 N4, Pearson Papers, vol. 1, file 001-42, Esmond Butler to Carl Lochnan, December 6, 1967.

135. Special Meeting of the Advisory Council, November 13, 1970.

136. CHAN, 708-3, Order of Canada Seal, Esmond Butler to Sir Michael Adeane, May 19, 1967.

137. CHAN, 708-3, file 1, Esmond Butler to Sir Michael Adeane, May 19, 1967.

138. CHAN, 708-3, Order of Canada Seal, Sir Michael Adeane to Esmond Butler, June 10, 1967.

139. Butler had Pearson sign the drawing prior to the prime minister attending a luncheon with the governor general. CHAN 708-3, Order of Canada Seal, Esmond Butler to J.S. Hodgson, June 20, 1967.

140. Charles Boutell, *English Heraldry* (London: Reeves & Turner, 1907), 179.

BIBLIOGRAPHY

Alexander, E.G.M., G.K.B. Barron, and A.J. Bateman. *South African Orders, Decorations and Medals*. Cape Town: Human & Rousseau, 1986.

Barber, Richard. *The Knight and Chivalry*. London: Longman, 1970.

Blatherwick, F.J. *Canadian Orders, Decorations, and Medals*. 3rd ed. Toronto: Unitrade, 1985.

Blondel, Jacques. *Guide Pratique des Décorations*. Paris: Lavauzelle, 1986.

Brass, Robin, and Wendy Thomas, eds. *The Register of Canadian Honours*. Toronto: Canadian Almanac and Directory, 1991.

Crook, M.J. *The Evolution of the Victoria Cross: A Study in Administrative History*. London: Midas Books, 1975.

De la Bere, Ivan. *The Queen's Orders of Chivalry*. London: William Kimber, 1961.

Fauteux, Aegidius. *Les Chevaliers de Saint-Louis en Canada*. Montreal: Éditions des Dix, 1940.

Ford, Frank. "Titles of Honour in Canada." *Queen's Quarterly* 10, no. 1 (1902).

Galloway, Peter. *Companions of Honour*. London: Third Millennium, 2002.

———. *The Most Illustrious Order of St. Patrick, 1783–1983*. Chichester: Phillimore, 1983.

———. *The Order of the Bath*. Chichester: Phillimore, 2006.

———. *The Order of the British Empire*. London: Spink, 1996.

———. *The Order of St Michael and St George*. London: Third Millennium, 2000.

———. *The Order of the Thistle*. London: Spink, 2009.

Galloway, Peter, David Stanley, and Stanley Martin. *Royal Service*. 3 vols. London: Third Millenium, 1996.

Gillingham, Harrold E. *French Orders and Decoration.* Numismatic Notes and Monographs 11. New York: American Numismatic Society, 1922.

Hayward, John, Diana Birch, and Richard Bishop. *British Battles and Medals.* 7th ed. London: Spink, 2006.

Lochnan, Carl. "History of Honours in Canada." Unpublished manuscript, 1976. Carl Lochnan Fonds, R5769. National Archives of Canada.

Martin, Stanley. *The Order of Merit: One Hundred Years of Matchless Honour.* London: I.B. Tauris, 2007.

McCreery, Christopher. *The Beginner's Guide to Canadian Honours.* Toronto: Dundurn, 2008.

———. *The Canadian Forces' Decoration.* Ottawa: DND, 2010.

———. *The Canadian Honours System.* Toronto: Dundurn, 2005.

———. *The Canadian Honours System.* 2nd ed. Toronto: Dundurn, 2015.

———. *Commemorative Medals of The Queen's Reign in Canada, 1952–2012.* Toronto: Dundurn, 2012.

———. "Honour, Nation and Citizenship in a Multicultural Polity: Federal Public Honours in Canada, 1917–1997." Doctoral thesis, Queen's University, 2003.

———. *Maintiens le Droit: Recognizing Service; A History of the RCMP Long Service Medal.* Ottawa: RCMP, 2014.

———. *The Maple Leaf and the White Cross: A History of St. John Ambulance and the Most Venerable Order of the Hospital of St. John of Jerusalem in Canada.* Toronto: Dundurn, 2008.

———. *On Her Majesty's Service: Royal Honours and Recognition in Canada.* Toronto: Dundurn, 2008.

———. *The Order of Canada: Its Origins, History, and Development.* Toronto: UTP, 2005.

———. *The Order of Military Merit.* Ottawa: DND, 2012.

———. "Questions of Honour: Canadian Government Policy Towards British Titular Honours, 1867–1935." Master's thesis, Queen's University, 1999.

Office of the Secretary to the Governor General. *Guide for the Wearing of Orders, Decorations and Medals.* Ottawa: Office of the Secretary to the Governor General, 2013.

Orders and Medals Research Society. *Journal of the Orders and Medals Research Society,* 1947–2013.

O'Shea, Phillip P., ed. *Honours, Titles, Styles and Precedence in New Zealand.* Wellington: Government Printer, 1977.

Taylor, Alister and Deborah Coddington. *Honoured by the Queen: New Zealand; Recipients of Honours, 1953-1993, and Royal Appointments to the Privy Council, as Queen's Counsel and as Justices of the Peace.* Auckland: New Zealand Who's Who Aotearoa, 1994.

Thomson, Donald Walter. "The Fate of Titles in Canada." *Canadian Historical Review* 10 (1929): 236–46.

IMAGE CREDITS

Author's Collection: 17 (top; bottom right), 18, 21, 23 (bottom), 25 (bottom), 27 (left and right), 32 (left and right), 34 (top), 38 (top right), 55 (top left; top right lower; bottom left; bottom middle; bottom right), 56 (all), 59, 60 (left and right), 61, 66 (bottom), 70, 73 (bottom left; bottom right upper, middle, and lower), 74, 75 (top and bottom), 76 (bottom), 77 (top and bottom), 78 (all), 79 (all), 80, 82, 94 (bottom), 95 (all), 96 (top left), 97 (top; bottom right), 98 (all), 99 (bottom), 100 (top left; bottom), 105 (top left and right), 108 (top), 109, 110 (top and bottom), 111 (right), 113, 115 (bottom), 116, 119, 122, 124 (top), 125 (top), 128 (all), 130 (all), 131 (top left and right), 132 (bottom left upper, middle, and lower; bottom right), 133, 141 (bottom), 142 (top right), 143 (bottom right), 150 (left and right).

Canadian Heraldic Authority: 42 (top), 44, 135 (left and right), 136 (all).

Canadian Press: 72 (top).

Chancellery of Honours: 52, 57 (bottom left, middle, and right), 145, 148 (top and bottom), 149 (top and bottom).

Department of Canadian Heritage: 6, 43 (top), 105 (bottom).

Department of National Defence: 15 (bottom), 16 (top; bottom left; bottom right), 17 (bottom left and centre), 26, 29, 34 (bottom), 37, 38 (top left; bottom),

39 (right), 83 (bottom), 84 (left and right), 86 (all), 96 (top right), 99 (top), 104 (left and right), 127 (bottom), 131 (middle; bottom right, middle, and left), 134 (right), 138 (all), 139 (all), 140 (all), 141 (top left and right; middle), 142 (bottom left), 143 (top left; middle right).

Esmond Butler Collection: 114 (top and bottom), 115 (top).

Hamilton Spectator Newspaper: 147.

Library and Archives Canada: 15 (top), 19 (top and bottom), 20 (all), 22 (top left; bottom), 24, 28, 30 (top left and right; bottom), 31, 33 (top), 35, 41, 43, 45, 46, 47, 51, 55 (top right upper), 64, 69, 72 (bottom left, middle, and right), 81, 85, 89, 94 (top), 97 (bottom right), 101, 102 (left), 108 (bottom), 120 (bottom), 121 (left and right), 123 (bottom), 125 (bottom), 126 (all middle, all bottom), 142 (top left), 143 (top middle and right; middle left), 146 (top and bottom).

National Film Board of Canada: 132 (top).

NATO Library: 126 (top).

Office of the Secretary to the Governor General: 7, 39 (left), 42 (bottom), 49, 53, 73 (top), 90 (top and bottom), 96 (bottom), 100 (top right), 102 (right), 103 (left and right), 106 (left and right), 111 (left), 120 (top), 123 (top), 134 (left and middle), 142 (bottom right), 143 (bottom right).

Provincial Archives of Nova Scotia: 76 (top).

Queen's University Archives: 22 (top right), 23 (top), 25 (top), 40, 67, 68 (all).

Senate of Canada: 57 (top).

Toronto Star: 147.

University of Manitoba Archives: 83 (top).

University of Toronto Archives: 33 (bottom), 36, 65, 66 (top right and left), 127 (top).

INDEX

Aarand, Argo, 95

Adeane, Sir Michael, 50, 52–54, 112

Advisory Council, 50–51, 56, 62, *64*, 65–66, *67*, 68, *69*, 70, 78, *87*, 109, 110, 111, 115, 119, 129, 134, *150*

Ahenakew, David, 91

Albani, Dame Emma, 24

Atholstan, 1ˢᵗ Baron, 21

Awards Coordination Committee, 27, 31, 35

Badgerow, Sir George Washington, 24

Banting, Sir Frederick, 24, *26*

baronetcies, 17, 21

Bassett, Douglas Graeme, *136*

Bathurst, 3rd Earl, 29

Batterwood, 46, 109

Beatty, Bruce, 14, 95, 97–98, *99*, 103, 106, *108*, *109*, 115, *116*, 117–18, *122*, 125, 129, 131, 133, 134, 137

Beauchemin, Micheline, 100

Beddoe, Alan , *120*, *121*, *123*, 127

Bennett, 1ˢᵗ Viscount (Richard Bedford Bennett), 23–24, *25*, 26, 40–41, 145

Best, Charles, 149

Black, Conrad, 91

Blackburn, Robert, 107

Borden, Sir Robert, 21, *22*, 23

bravery decorations, 18, 81, 85, 95, 117

British Empire Medal, *98*, 109

British honours system, 17–18

Brown, E.F., 95

Bryant, Joyce, 14, 65, *83*, *98*, *99*, 100, 106, *108, 109, 110, 111*, 115, 124, *127*

Buckingham, N.A., 117

Butler, Esmond, 14, 35, *42*, 46–52, *53*, 54, *57*, 58, *59*, 62, *64*, 65, 71, 79, 98, *99*, 107, *108*, 109–10, *111*, 112, *113*, *114*, *115*, 134, 150

Callaghan, Morley, 77

Cameron, Dean, *136*

Canada Gazette, 61, 69, *72*, *102*, 134

Canada Medal, 28, 31, *32*, 38, 44, 48–49, 58, 60, 133

Canadian Armed Forces, *34*, 81, 82, 84–85, 87, 117, *122*

Canadian Army, 28, 38, 117

Canadian Award of Honour, 27, 120, *123*, 124, 127

Canadian Decoration of Honour, 27, *120*, *121*, 124, 127

Canadian Expeditionary Force, 21

Canadian flag, 40–41, 123

Canadian Forces. *See* Canadian Armed Forces

Canadian Forces' Decoration, *34*, 87

Canadian Heraldic Authority, 92, 103, 135

Canadian Military. *See* Canadian Armed Forces

Centennial of Confederation, 11, 37, 43, 48, 50, 54, 59–60, 71–72, *73*, 87, 109, 117, *146*

Centennial Medal, 37, *38*, *39*, 51

Chancellery of Honours, 85, 92, 93, 109, 111, *122*, 134

chancellor's chain, 95, *96*

Chapais, Sir Thomas, 25

Chung, Young Sup, 136

Clerk of the Privy Council, 48, 49, 54, 56, *57*, 58, *64*, 65, 69, 75, 107

Coldwell, M.J., 61, 75

Coleman, Ephriam, 31, 120

College of Arms, 92, 108, 121

colonial secretary, 18, 29

Colville, Alex, 106

Comfort, Charles, *30*, *125*

Commonwealth, 18, 30, 37, 59, 95, 113, 124, 133

Confederation, 11, 18, 37, 48, 85, 87, 102, *103*, *104*, 133

Cornwall and York, Duke and Duchess of, *19*. *See also* George V, King

Coronation Medal, *38*

Cross of Valour, 81, *86*

Crown, institution, 13, 18, 37, *47*, *53*, *57*, *73*, 87, 92, 113, 114

Cudmore, Evelyn, 149

Department of National Defence, 34, 37, 51, 53, 84, 108, 116, 120, 125, *126*, 127

Department of the Secretary of State, 85

Diefenbaker, John George, *35*, 37, 41, 58, 75, *99*, 112, 123

Distinguished Conduct Medal, 18

Distinguished Flying Cross, *17*, 18

Distinguished Service Cross, 53

Doughty, Sir Arthur, 25

Drabinsky, Garth, 91, 149

Drapeau, Jean, 149

Eagleson, Alan, 91, 149

Edinburgh, Duke of, 71, *90*, 91, 93

Edward VII, King, 37

Elizabeth, Queen Mother, 89

Elizabeth II, Queen, 6, 18, 37, *47*, 49, 50, *51*, *52*, *53*, 54, 56, 58, 59, 61, 68, 71, *72*, *73*, 75, *80*, *83*, 87, 91, 93, *94*, *95*, 98, *99*, 102, 103, 107, 112, 113, 115, 119, 127, 129, 134

Ethell, Donald, *135*

Exemplary Service Medals, 87, 117

Expo 67, 11, *73*, *99*, *146*

Fedoruk, Sylvia Olga, *135*

First World War, 13, 18–20, *41*, *47*, 63, 79, 101, 112, 149

Fonyo, Stephen, 91

Forsey, Eugene, 149

Fox, Terry, 101, *102*, 149

Franklin, Ursula, 149

Frontenac, Count, 16

Fulton, Davie, 57

Gélinas, Gaetan, 61

George V, King, *18*, 19, 26, 37, 87, 124

George VI, King, 22, 26, *34*, 37

George Cross, 53, 80

George, David Lloyd, 21

George Medal, 18, 80

Genest, Jacques, 106

Government Decorations Committee, 34–35, 56

Government House. *See also* Rideau Hall

governor general, *7*, 11, 13, 18–21, *29*, 30, 31, 32, 35, *36*, 44, 46, *47*, 48, *49*, *53*,

54, 56, *57*, 58, 62, 63, 65, 68–69, 71, *73*, 75, *85*, 88, *90*, 91, 93, 95, *96*, *98*, *99*, 100–4, *105*, *106*, 107–8, *109*, 110, *111*, 112–14, 120, 124, 129, 134, 140

Graham, Sir Hugh. *See* Atholstan, 1ˢᵗ Baron

Halstead, John, 14, 107, *126*, 127
Hellyer, Paul, 37, *38*, 51
Herzberg, Gerhard, 65, *67*
Hnatyshyn, Ramon, 104, 108
Hodgson, John S. (Jack), 47, 107, 125, 131, *132*, 150
honour, concept of, 13, 15, 25, *36*, 150
Hughes, Sir Sam, 21

imperial honours, 17, 18, 20, 26, 27, 29, 31, 39, 40, 63, 80
Imperial Service Order, 28
investiture, 13, 24, *36*, 62, 71, 72, 73, 76, 89, 93, 95, *99*, 100–2, 104, 107, 111, 113, 115, 118, 123, *132*

Jean, Michaëlle, *106*
Johnston, David, *90*, 93, *96*
Joslin, E.C., 124

Karsh, Yousuf, 149
King, William Lyon Mackenzie, *24*, 26, 28, *30*, 31, 32, 35, 40, 41, 51, 58, *64*, 88, *121*
knighthood, 18, 20–23, 29
Korean War, 28, 34

Lafond, Jean-Daniel, *106*
LaMarsh, Judy, 51, 58
Laurier, Sir Wilfrid, *19*, *20*
Leblanc, Guy, 44
LeBlanc, Roméo, *109*
Léger, Cardinal, 149
Léger, Jules, *94*, 95
Légion d'honneur, 14, 84, 121, 130, *131*
Letson, H.F.G., 31, 120
letters patent, 52, 54, 56, 57, 58, *83*, 107
Lévesque, Georges-Henri, *33*, 63, 75
Lewis, David, 58

Library of Parliament, 46, *128*
lieutenant governor, 24, 101
Lochnan, Carl, 80
Longueuil, Baron de, *15*, 16
Louis XIV, King, *16*
Lower, Arthur, *68*, *70*

MacDonald, Edythe, 52, 54, *83*, 107
MacDonald, Flora, 88
McGibbon, Pauline, 149
Mackenzie, Norman, *33*, 63
McLean, John Ross, *45*
MacMillan, Sir Ernest, 25, 101
McTeer, Maureen, *89*
Mandela, Nelson, 89
Maple Leaf flag, 43, 107
Martin, Paul, Jr., *136*
Martin, Paul, Sr., 51
Martineau, Jean, 63
Mary, Queen, 19
Massey Commission, *33*, *34*, 36, 63, 75. *See also* Royal Commission on the National Development of the Arts, Letters and Sciences
Massey, Vincent, 13–14, *30*, 31–32, *33*, *36*, 39, *40*, *41*, *42*, 44, *45*, 46–48, *49*, 50, *53*, *57*, 61, 63, 65, *66*, 75, *98*, *99*, 107, 109, 110, 112, 120, 124, *127*, 150
Matheson, John, 14, 39, *40*, *41*, *42*, 43, 46–50, 52, *57*, 107, 120, 122, *124*, *126*, *127*, *128*, 150
Medal of Bravery, 81, *86*
Medal of Courage. *See under* Order of Canada
Medal of Service. *See under* Order of Canada
Meighen, Arthur, 24
Meritorious Service Cross, 87
Meritorious Service Medal, 87
Michener, Norah, *73*
Michener, Roland, *7*, *61*, 71, *72*, *73*, 74–76, *85*, 95, 97–98, *99*, 101, 103, *105*, 107, 110, 134
Military. *See* Canadian Armed Forces
Military Cross, *17*, 18, 53, 133
Military Medal, 18

Minto, 4th Earl of, 19, *20*

Monck, 4th Viscount, *29*, 30, 33, 120

Montgomery, Lucy Maud, 25

Morgentaler, Henry, *147*, 149

Nakaya, Ukichiro, *119*, 125, *128*, 129, 150

Nantel, Roger de C., 80, 107–08, 110

Neatby, Hilda, *33*, 63

Nickle Resolution, 22–24, 39, *42*

Nickle, William Folger, *22*, 23, 24, 39–40, *42*, 150

North Atlantic Treaty Organization (NATO), 34, 87, 107, 116, *126*, 127

O'Driscoll, Herbert, 122

Ondaatje, Sir Christopher, *136*

Order of the Bath, 17, 21, 28, 84

Order of the Beaver, 27, 31, 121

Order of the British Empire, 17, 21, 23–25, 28, 40, *41*, 80–81

Order of Canada

    Insignia, 13–14, 48, *52*, 53, *55*, 69, 71, *72*, 74, *77*, *78*, 93, 95, 98, *99*, 100, 101, 103, 104, 106, 107, *115*, 116, 117, 118, 119, *120*, 121, *122*, 123–27, *128*, 129, *130*, 131–36, 137–43, *144*, *145*

    Lapel Badge, 130, *131*, *132*, 133

    Medal of Courage, 53–54, *55*, 56, 58, 80–81, 129, *131*, 133

    Medal of Service, 11, 54, *56*, 58, *64*, 66, 72, 74–75, *76*, 77–78, *87*, 95, 104, 129, *131*, 133

    Register, 74, *90*, *149*

    Registrar, 48, 108, 110

    Resignations, 91, 110

    Ribbon, 13, *42*, 107, 119, 123, *124*, *125*, 130, *132*, 133, 138, 140

    Terminations, 91, 134

Order of the Garter, *99*, 121, 135

Order of Merit, 27, 30, 48, *99*, 124

Order of Merit of the Police Forces, 85, 93, *96*, 135

Order of Military Merit, 81, *82*, *83*, 84, *85*, 93, 95, *96*, 100, *115*, 117, *126*, 135, 137

Order of St. Lawrence, 27, *29*, 30, 31, 33–34, *36*, 64, 120

Order of St. Louis, *16*

Order of St. Michael and St. George, *17*, 24, 28, 29, 30

Order of the Star of India, 29

Parliament, *19*, 20, 23, 27, 35, 41, 44, 46, 64, 72, 74, 112, 123, *128*

Pearkes, George, 61, 65

Pearson, Lester B., 14, 25, 35, 37–40, *41*, *42*, 43, 44, *45*, *46*, 47–52, 54, *57*, *58*, 60, 71, 74, 76, 78, 81, 85, 93, 107, 117, 121, 123, 124, 125, 129, 130, *132*, 134, 150

Penfield, Wilder, *99*

Perlin, John C., *136*

Philip, Prince. *See* Edinburg, Duke of

Pitfield, Michael, 14, *42*, 47–49, 50, 57, *64*, 79, 107, 110, 121, 150

police, 53, 54, 85, 87

Queen Elizabeth II Coronation Medal, *38*

Red Ensign flag, 35, 41, *42*

Report of the Special Committee on Honours and Titles, 23

Richard, Maurice, 61

Rideau Hall, *53*, 58, 65, 66, 69, 71, 72, *73*, 74, 93, *94*, 95, *98*, *101*, *103*, 104, 106, 108–15. *See also* Government House

Rigaud, Pierre de, *16*

Robertson, Gordon, 14, 54, *57*, 58, *64*, 65, 107, 150

Robertson, Norman A., 75

Royal Arms of Canada, 97, 103, *105*, 122, 124, 125

Royal Canadian Air Force (RCAF), *17*, 28, 38, *98*, 108, 109, 116, 117, *122*

Royal Canadian Horse Artillery, 39, *42*

Royal Canadian Mint, 95, 100, 106, 117, *120*, 137, *142*, *143*, *144*

Royal Canadian Mounted Police (RCMP). *See* RCMP Long Service Medal

RCMP Long Service Medal, *18*, 26, *27*, *28*, 87

Royal Canadian Naval Volunteer Reserve, *53*, 112, *126*, *132*

Royal Canadian Navy, 28, 38, *99*, 108, 117

Royal Commission on the National Development of the Arts, Letters and Sciences, 33, *36*, 45, 48, 63–64, 75, 120. *See also* Massey Commission

Royal Commission on Spying Activities, *69*

Royal Military College, *42*

Royal Order of Canada, 27, *30*, 31, 120, *125*

Royal Prerogative, 59

Royal Society of Canada, 49, 56, 65, *67*, 70

Royal Tour, *19*, 71, *72*, 112, 117

Royal Victorian Order, 20, *53*, *57*, 85, 114, 127

Royal Visit. *See* Royal Tour

Royal Warrant, *28*

St. Laurent, Louis, 33, 41, 64, 66, 75, *99*

Schreyer, Edward, *64*, 95, 101

Scott, F.R., 77

Second World War, 18, 26, 27, 28, 39–40, *41*, *42*, 47, *53*, 63, 82, 88, *98*, 101, 108, *121*, *122*, 126, *132*

secretary to the governor general, 31, 35, 49, 53, 56, 65, 71, 85, 98, 107, 110, 111, 112, 114, 120

Shaughnessy, Sir Thomas, 19–20

Sheardown, Zena, 88, *89*

Singh, T. Sher, 91

Skyline Hotel, 72

Smyth, Anthony (Tony), 106, 107

snowflake, 13, *77*, 97, 117–18, 119–20, 125, *126*, 127, *128*, 129–30, 137, 140, 142, 150

Sovereign's Badge and insignia, 95, *97*, 98, 103, *115*

Special Committee on Honours and Awards, 31

Special Committee on Honours and Decorations, 48

Special Committee on Honours and Titles, 23

Stanfield, Robert, 75

Stanley, George, *40*, 42

Star of Courage, 81, *86*

Star of Military Valour, 87

Stephenson, Sir William, 101

Summers, William, 97, 137

Surveyor, Arthur, *33*, 63

Swan, Sir Conrad, 108, 121, 130

Taschereau, Robert, 58, 65, *69*

Taylor, Patricia, *89*

Tehran, 88–89

Trudeau, Pierre, *64*, 85

Tunis, Viscount Alexander of, 32, *33*, 34, 88, 109, 120, 124

Tweedsmuir, 1st Baron (John Buchan), 30

Vanier, Georges, 11, 35, *45*, *46*, *47*, 49–50, *53*, 54, 56, 58, *73*, 112, 129

Vanier, Pauline, 11, *47*, 61, 65, 75

Victoria Cross, 18, 53, 87, 133

Victoria, Queen, 37

Washington, George, 17

Working Group on Honours, 79–81

dundurn.com
@dundurnpress
dundurnpress
dundurnpress
dundurnpress
info@dundurn.com

FIND US ON NetGalley & GOODREADS TOO!

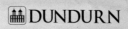 DUNDURN